For my mother, who showed me that having
a warm and well-kept home can enhance your life.

For my father, who set me free into a world
of words and books. *Tempus fugit!*

And for Daniel, who has helped to create all of
our many homes. And made this book possible.
Thank you.

THIS IS HOME

THE ART OF SIMPLE LIVING

NATALIE WALTON

Photography by Chris Warnes

Hardie Grant

BOOKS

one

Create

Live

Nurture

HOW TO MAKE A HOME

1. DEVELOP A SENSE OF STYLE

2. FOCUS ON STORY

3. MANAGE PRIORITIES

4. ELEVATE FUNCTION

5. CREATE TRUE BEAUTY

6. APPEAL TO THE SENSES

7. CONNECT TO THE SURROUNDING SPACES

8. STAY FOCUSED

9. BE ADAPTABLE

10. NURTURE YOURSELF

INTRODUCTION

This is a love story about the home.
It celebrates what we have.
And reminds us to nurture the space that helps make our lives possible.

What makes a home? It seems like a simple question but the answer is a little more complex. In many ways, homes embody how we live and see ourselves. And these spaces evolve when we focus on what makes us happy. This is sometimes easier said than done, though. It requires reflection and thoughtful choices, but it is a rewarding process. When we create a place that meets our needs on many levels, and expresses our character, we can enrich our lives.

These ideas have emerged while working for more than ten years in the interiors industry – first as a writer, and then as a stylist and former deputy editor of a homes magazine, and more recently as a designer and shopkeeper. During this time I've seen hundreds, if not thousands, of residences – across all spectrums. What I've learnt is that when you walk into some homes they instantly feel welcoming. Not only do you want to be there but part of you doesn't want to leave. And it's not just because you enjoy the company or admire the decor – although both help – but there's something else. The space feels authentic, a genuine reflection of the person or family who lives there.

Homes that have a strong sense of identity often belong to people who are thoughtful with all that they do. That's not to say you need lots of money or status to create a beautiful home. In fact, many of the homes in this book belong to people who live quiet lives. But they have been considered in their choices. And they have made decisions based on *their* needs and what works in *their* home. Because it makes them happy. It brings them contentment and joy. It makes them feel calm and comfortable. And having a home that meets their needs means that they can turn their focus onto other realms, from raising a family, building a business, developing an art practice, travelling the world, indulging a hobby or creating another home.

For this book, I have travelled across four continents and seven countries, and stepped inside more than twenty residences, to see if there is some universality to the idea of home and what makes us happy in our spaces. The people on the following pages have different needs and resources but have all created authentic homes where they can enjoy both the simplest and grandest gestures of life.

Some of them have created the foundations of a home quite quickly because it was important for them to be surrounded by pieces that had meaning and brought comfort, especially when living in a city or country far removed from their own. Some have created unique and effective solutions for their space precisely because they didn't have an infinite budget. And others have allowed themselves the luxury of time – slowly and thoughtfully adding to their collections over the years – perhaps an item found while on travels or something that was saved for and happily moved from one dwelling to another.

While every home in this book is a living example of a warm and genuine space, these homes also shine a light on what happens when we focus on what we value – we can create our best spaces.

***

On page 7 are my ten foundations for creating an authentic and wholehearted space. They don't have to be followed sequentially – often the concepts overlap and reinforce one another. And just like a home, this is not a process that 'ends'. Homes always need to change and adapt, and the more that we engage with the process of decision-making, curating and arranging, the better we get at it. I hope the homes and stories in this book remind us that when we focus on what makes us happy, we can create a life of meaning. And that can begin at home.

‹ The author Natalie Walton at work in her home in the Yarramalong Valley of NSW, Australia.

'We expect our homes to function in many ways today, we also want them to feel more human, more us.'

Ilse Crawford

one

CREATE

EVOLUTION

EXPRESSION

PRIORITIES

CREATE

A home is one of our most important creations. Within its frame, we create lifelong memories and manage our lives. It is where we wake and set the tone for the rest of our day, as well as nourish our bodies. At the day's end, we decompress, shed the layers of social complexities and maybe even lick our wounds. Within its rooms, we restore our bodies – on the sofa, in the bath, in bed. Our home is much more than a shelter from the elements. It is a space that needs to function on many levels but it's also our most intimate space to *feel*. Safe. Secure. Protected. Nurtured. Loved. It is a place where we can be ourselves. ———— It is no wonder that we invest a lot of time, money and emotion into creating our home. Not only in finding the right place but in trying to make it meet our needs. However, somewhere along that journey from dreaming to making, we can become stuck or sidetracked. Options can seem endless. Decisions can weigh heavily. And we can become unsure of which direction to take. ———— But when we focus on our values, decision-making becomes easy. The weight of choosing is lifted when we embrace our story. And when we listen to our inner voice, we find our way.

'If one advances in the direction of his dreams, and endeavors to live the life which he has imagined, he will meet with a success unexpected in common hours ... If you have built castles in the air, your work need not be lost; that is where they should be. Now put the foundations under them.'
Henry David Thoreau

EVOLUTION

There are few words as evocative as 'home'. It conjures visions of our ideal sanctuary. A happy place, filled with beauty, harmony and love. We tell ourselves that if we could just make it perfect, whatever we take that to mean, then life would be so too. But it's a misnomer, of course. A home is more vital and nuanced than that. It is a work in progress, reflecting and adapting to the changes in our lives. If we think of our home as ever-evolving, mistakes are nothing to fear. They are how we learn and improve, and they become part of the stories that help to make our home authentic.

The idea of home has come a long way. The form that we recognise today can be traced back to the Netherlands in the seventeenth century. Prior to that, dwellings tended to be communal spaces that accommodated large groups of people who lived, worked, and slept together. When the Dutch embarked on their prosperous Golden Age, they started to redefine our idea of home. As money and time became more readily available, they developed places that focused on family needs and created rooms that were used for just one function instead of many.

All over the world, whenever wealth and security grows and survival is no longer the primary concern, we have the opportunity to consider our own individual wants. However, we can feel a tension between being part of a social tribe and aligning our homes with a look, while finding a way to express our individual sense of self. But when we discover our 'voice', or sense of style, we embark on a lifelong journey of living authentically. And we can create a home that enhances our lives.

'For our house is our corner of the world ...
It is our first universe, a real cosmos in every sense of the word.'
Gaston Bachelard

Develop
a sense of style

It is easy to become attached to the idea of creating a certain 'look' at home. But a home is more complex than that. And so are we.

A sense of style evolves through the prism of our values. And when we let these be our guide, a visual voice emerges that's fluid and permeable, and can adapt to the constant changes that are an inevitable part of life. It means that we don't have to overhaul our homes every couple of years, which wastes time and resources. After all, looks are dated as soon as they are created. Instead, we have a way of seeing the world and making decisions that can contribute to a unique home.

Values

If our values can help guide many of life's decisions, how do we work out what they are? And what do we prioritise? A value is something that is important to us, such as family, community, sustainability, beauty, authenticity, nature, and so on. These are often deep-rooted beliefs that shape our lives. When it comes to our homes, focusing on what we value can help answer some of the big questions such as where to live and whether we decorate or renovate, and how we allocate our available funds. Our values can also guide the types of spaces we create. Do we want to prioritise quality, simplicity, artistry or innovation? While these values don't have to be mutually exclusive, they provide a decision-making framework for the materials we choose, the plans we draw up, and the atmosphere we create.

Trust

At the start of any project, information gathering plays an important role. However, there comes a point when we benefit from setting aside inspirational images and finding our own way. This is when we need to learn to trust ourselves. Part of this comes from experience but, over time, it becomes instinctive. And we learn to trust the process too. When a project is too focused on the end result, there is little room for serendipity or happy accidents. And few spaces look their best when first finished – they benefit from the layers that come with life.

Curiosity

There is a lot to be gained from curiosity. Not only can we learn more about our interests, but it is a way to push our creative boundaries. When we talk to experts, we learn more about products, process and possibilities. While we can design spaces from a desk, we benefit from the experience of touching materials and talking to skilled artisans who work with them every day.

Individuality

Temptation is always in our way though. New products. Old products marketed in new ways. Trends. Theories. The cult of people and places. We need to wade through all of this to stay true to ourselves. However, when we have a clear idea of what we value, trends fall into insignificance. When we see how others have decorated their home, we can appreciate it but we don't feel an urge to replicate it. When we are surrounded by limitless choice and a constant stream of ideas, our values create a roadmap that is uniquely our own.

Ameé Allsop

'Home is a constant river of creativity. It is forever changing and growing, pushing you to be better and take stock of where you are. It is embedded with memories and dreams, tangible and intangible. It is personal and universal. It is a safe space.'

THERE'S A BIG DIFFERENCE between living in a 'treehouse' in Whale Beach, north of Sydney, Australia, and a loft in the New York borough of Brooklyn. 'But we were ready for a change of scale,' says architect Ameé Allsop of the move she made to America with her photographer husband, Glen Allsop. 'I had dreams of living in a loft building. They are just not common in Australia so why not live the New York dream?'

After Glen was offered work shooting for a photography studio in Manhattan the couple made the move and started hunting for homes in Williamsburg. They were keen on the neighbourhood because of its views across the East River and the prevalence of good coffee shops and a community of creative types. Tracking down a suitable residence in New York can be fraught though. 'In New York, it feels like finding treasure when you find "your place",' Ameé says. 'It is the first thing people ask when you meet them. "Where do you live?" and "Where are you from?"'

When the couple first arrived in Brooklyn, Ameé was always on the lookout for loft buildings and one day saw a small sign with a landlord's phone number. The place hadn't been advertised yet and the couple had their lucky moment. They instantly fell for the building and its high ceilings, concrete floors, large factory-style windows to the south, and its open-plan kitchen. 'The scale of it allowed us to breathe in a city that is compact and at times suffocating,' she says.

It's been six years since they moved into the loft. Since then they have put up a couple of walls and glass French doors to create two bedrooms, and painted over a purple feature wall. Most importantly, they added a third member to their family, their three-year-old son, Navy. The space has adapted since his arrival and created a sense of home for them. 'Which is important since we are not in our homeland,' Ameé says. 'Our home is a big part of why we have stayed six years in one place already and plan on staying longer. There are friends who have come and gone, and all for different reasons, but I believe a big part of it is whether or not they were able to find a place that they could call home.'

The loft has been a flexible space, and enabled them to adapt to their expanded family life. Previously a large part of the living room was a dedicated office space for both of them but now the desks have been removed and an extra sofa added to allow for more room to relax at home and for Navy to play. The living area is now Ameé's favourite space. 'It has taken a while to get it how it is, which is fulfilling,' she says.

Ameé Allsop

How do you choose which items enter your home?
In the early days we were on a tight budget and so I made a lot of the furniture. We still have the bed I made in our loft during a storm. And plywood benches and shelves. It's a matter of space and longevity.

How often do you edit your home and its collections?
We don't have much storage space and definitely no garage so we don't accumulate much, but we also edit quite regularly. Mainly smaller items, such as clothes, homewares, magazines, toys.

What's involved in the process?
With editing, think 'spring clean'. Plan a bigger change with new furniture, some sketches, a tape measure, a lot of thinking and conversation.

What objects hold a special meaning for you?
Mostly the artworks – Glen's photographs, Navy's paintings, and others from Australia and Copenhagen. But also a stool from a trip to Formentera, some stones I collected from the beach with Navy, brass candleholders from Stockholm, a Flensted mobile. Lastly, the first two sofas we purchased – a black leather Chesterfield, then a white Belgian linen modular sofa – the perfect combination of NY and Sydney in my mind.

How has your style evolved over the years?
What has stayed consistent?
I believe my approach to space, objects and materials has stayed the same. However, the focus and patience for finding the items that will last has developed.

Which materials are important to you?
Quality and natural materials.

What gets priority in your home?
Living. It used to be work but now it is about creating a space where we can rest after busy days in this fast-paced city.

When are you happy at home?
When Navy is playing, Glen has got his feet up on the sofa, red wine, afternoon or sunset light is streaming in, music is playing, dinner is in the oven. Or when Glen is playing the piano with Navy and I'm reading with feet up on the sofa. Or when Navy is asleep on the sofa and Glen and I are chatting about the future with our feet up on the sofa. Or when we have friends over for drinks (Negronis) and cheese, and Navy is jumping all over the sofa making us laugh. Many scenarios – but usually including feet up on the sofa. We walk a lot in this city!

What do you think makes a welcoming home?
The small details: a clean and tidy home, items considerately placed, a touch of handmade, original artwork, nice scents, music, light and laughter – to name a few.

'Too much waste is created these days by things that are not made to last. We'd rather wait, save more money and buy something that is made well – with natural materials – that will last a long time. This goes for the design as well. It needs to be simple and timeless, not trendy. It is not only more cost-effective in the long run but better for the environment. We feel the same way about clothing.'

Ameé

EXPRESSION

Our home is a way of expressing how we see ourselves. It is a place where we can test out ideas about how we want to live, and who we want to be. Within our walls we have the freedom to create, play and think. No one is watching. But who are we? And how can we create a home if we aren't always sure? Or change our minds? It's simple but perhaps not easy – we need to become ourselves.

The desire to reach our full potential is on top of the pyramid of human needs. Psychologist Abraham Maslow developed his seminal theory, the Hierarchy of Needs, in the middle of the twentieth century. The idea is that once our base human needs are met – air, water, food, clothing and shelter – and we feel safe and loved, we can reach a level of self-acceptance. Then we can focus on reaching our full potential; 'to become everything that one is capable of becoming'.

Homes that have a strong sense of identity – which is different to having a strong look – belong to people who have a clear sense of who they are and what they want. They are not trying to emulate someone else's style or follow trends. They have a vision of what they want of their home and they focus on achieving it.

When we accept who we are and embrace our own story we can create a place that makes us feel good. And at this point our homes can be whatever we want them to be.

'All men have a sense of what is right ... if they would only use and apply this sense; every man knows where and how beauty gives him pleasure, if he would only ask for it when he does so, and not allow it to be forced upon him when he does not want it.'

John Ruskin

Focus on story

If our home can be anything we want it to be, are we happy with what we have created? Does it tell our story? Homes feel genuine when we focus on what's important. We create meaningful environments when our spaces highlight what we value, elevate everyday tasks and stir our memories.

However, we need to allow space for the future too. Homes are our story in 3D form, and there needs to be room for the next chapter. When everything is resolved in one sweeping gesture, we exist only in that moment. When a level of 'perfection' has been attained, how can we add to it? Homes need to be fluid so they can evolve. When they are created slowly, they can breathe. Our story is a continual work in progress, and our homes should be too.

Play

Our home can be one of our most expressive creations. For some of us, it's our most creative form of art-making since childhood. Play is an important but sometimes overlooked element in our lives. However, when we engage in it we can learn about ourselves, as well as experience joy. Einstein took regular breaks from his work to play the violin, a practice he said helped stimulate new ideas. And Picasso devoted his career to creating with child-like wonder. When we engage in forms of play, such as art-making, we can express ourselves in new ways. As artist Georgia O'Keeffe said, she was able to communicate via forms and colours in ways that she couldn't through words. Creating a home is also a powerful way to express ourselves and meet many of our needs.

History

When we create a home we should consider the former life of the building or site. When we elevate connections to the past, we enrich the story of our own place. We also feel a greater connection to our community when we create or maintain a building that's sympathetic to its surrounds. But honouring the past doesn't need to be at the expense of making our home comfortable or enjoying modern conveniences. We can celebrate the features that attracted us to the building, such as high ceilings, timber flooring or marble fireplaces, but within the context of what we need for contemporary living.

Connect

Objects that tell stories or evoke memories can create and enhance important emotional connections in our home. When we become interested in the layers of how something is made, it becomes a more valuable part of our lives. Learning about the maker, their process and the product's journey can enrich our experience when we see and touch it at home. When we embrace handmade and artisanal wares, craftsmanship, and vintage pieces, we connect to a human story, and weave it with our own.

Simone McEwan
& Patrik Bergh

LONDON, UK

'For us, to create a home is to create a sanctuary for our family.
A home that can evolve and grow over time. It should feel inherently warm and welcoming.'

THERE'S A PALPABLE ENERGY in the home of Simone McEwan and Patrik Bergh. Part of it relates to their two young active boys, Hunter, nine, and Viggo, six, but also to the couple, who enjoy animated conversation and embrace the creative path they have chosen. Walls are filled with art, and shelves with books, and colour is used confidently.

The couple's North London home absorbs the full force of life. It can act as a place for football games, headstands, band practice, art class, science experiments and dancing competitions. 'Keeping up with our children means our home needs to be adaptable, flexible, durable and certainly not precious,' says Simone. While she trained as an architect in her native Australia, most of her career has been spent working as an interior designer. Currently creative director at one of the world's leading design firms (which takes a humanist approach), it's something that's always been a thread in her own life and work. It's a sentiment that Patrik, a filmmaker originally from Sweden, shares.

'We passionately believe that a home should be real, honest and full of soul,' Simone says. 'We don't feel comfortable in a space that is over designed, devoid of character and sterile in personality. The essence of a home is what makes you feel good, who you are. Ultimately there has to be an emotional connection, creating spaces that are enjoyable, friendly and comfortable, and make us happy.'

The couple bought the house almost ten years ago after they had their first child and wanted to upgrade to a family home. They had been living in the area for a long time and often walked past this row of terrace houses and admired their historic details and design. Traditional London Victorian houses are often quite narrow and long and have a kitchen at the back that's disconnected from the front living rooms. 'The terrace houses on this street are Edwardian, which are wider, feel more spacious internally and the internal spaces are more connected,' Simone says. An existing open kitchen and dining room was one of the key features that appealed to the couple.

Simone and Patrik took the idea of inclusion one step further and installed a pair of original French glazed doors to create a connection between the dining and living room. 'Both Patrik and I are used to living in open-plan spaces so for us it was important to regain a feeling of space,' Simone says. The doors mean that they can close off the rooms to provide some separation when needed.

They were keen to retain some of the home's character by keeping its original beautiful features, such as cornices, doors and skirting, but adding their own layers too. The couple hunted down reclaimed oak flooring from an old school gymnasium and sourced Moroccan cement tiles to introduce colour and pattern.

'We always consider and respect the history of the building, to enhance any original features and material palette, but layering our own story and history through the decoratives, books and art,' Simone says. 'To create light, comfortable spaces layered with modernity and texture.'

What objects hold a special meaning for you?
We are lucky to have inherited a couple of very precious artworks from Patrik's father who was an avid art collector, and some beautiful Swedish glass items from Patrik's mother who, ahead of her time, opened London's first Swedish design shop in the 1980s. Along with these my mother, who is an artist, has given me some of her small maquette sculptures, which I absolutely love.

How do you choose which items enter your home?
There is definitely no real strategy. Any furniture or decoratives that we purchase for the house are things that we emotionally connect to. But much to Patrik's annoyance, there are way too many chairs entering our house.

How often do you edit your home and its collections?
Our house is small, so space is at a premium, and it can get cluttered very easily. Because of this we have to constantly edit. Any new purchases generally mean something needs to be compromised and recycled. We consider any new additions carefully, making sure it's something we want to invest in and thinking about where it will sit.

How has your style evolved over the years?
I am more confident with colour than I used to be when I was younger. Experience and age have given me more confidence to apply colour through furniture. We have always been passionate about investing in vintage pieces, which are inherently full of character and personality.

Which materials are important to you?
Real, natural materials that can age. I have tested many types of materials within my design work and through our home. The things that always last and feel good are the materials that are natural. Other choices we have made over the years due to budget and trend, have either scratched, chipped, stained, and just don't stand the wear and tear of everyday life. It's better to invest in the materials that you touch, feel and use.

What gets priority in your home?
Scents. We try to make sure the house smells fresh. It's easy for London houses to smell damp so we are obsessed with good smells. We also love soft ambient lighting, so low-level floor and table lamps are a priority. As well as an abundance of candles during the dark winter months.

What's your favourite space?
The dining room. The table is at the heart of our house. It connects the living room and the kitchen. It brings us all together. We use this space all day, every day.

When are you happy at home?
I am always happiest when the sun is shining and we can have all the doors to the garden open.

What do you think makes a welcoming home?
A feeling of warmth and informality. By not over-designing a space and making it real, it has a feeling of who you are and how you live. It gives any guest an immediate sense of comfort and feeling of ease.

Caitlin & Samuel Dowe-Sandes

MARRAKECH, MOROCCO

'A home, our home, is an emblem for all that is important. Family and sustenance – food and sleep and love. It's where we put out the objects and art, arranged in a fashion that reflects who we are and what we value, maybe even what we hope to become. A house is an accumulation of things and experiences and people, but home goes deeper and is more personal. I like what Alain de Botton said: "What we call a home is merely any place that succeeds in making more consistently available to us the important truths which the wider world ignores, or which our distracted and irresolute selves have trouble holding onto."'

THE IDEA OF HOME can take on a several meanings when you are living in a foreign country. For Caitlin Dowe-Sandes, the co-founder of tiling company Popham Designs with her husband, Samuel, the notion of home is entwined with where she comes from – Maine, on the north-east coast of the USA. 'Maybe this attachment to the place where I grew up is exacerbated by having lived as an expat for eleven years,' she says. 'But for me, nothing captures the elemental sense of "home" and security and grounding that I feel when I touch down at Boston's Logan airport every summer, breathe in that cool, fresh-cut-grass-laced air and wend my way up north on a forested highway to Maine. I can feel my body relaxing into New England the way I relax into my husband's neck.' However, the home she has made with her family, which includes seven-year-old daughter Georgina, is in Marrakech. The couple moved to the Moroccan city after living for eight years in Los Angeles, where Samuel worked in film and Caitlin in PR, mainly for design businesses and restaurants. They crossed the Atlantic for a year-long sabbatical

that morphed into launching Popham Design ten years ago. Over that time they have lived in two other houses, the first of which was in the medina. But their preference is to live in what is considered the 'new' town, Gueliz, which was built by the French in the early 1900s. They enjoy the convenience of being able to drive up to their front door and be within walking distance of the area's modern conveniences. 'With a kiddo and a big labrador retriever, the in-town location, as opposed to the medieval maze of the medina, was a welcome change,' she says.

The house that they found also gave them an opportunity to experiment with their designs, and have a little fun in their home. Ultimately, though, they wanted to create a sanctuary. 'Since we moved to Marrakech, we've always regarded our homes as a reprieve from the nutty energy of Marrakech, be it the medina or new town,' Caitlin says. 'We adore this energy and feed off it creatively but, just as your body needs some deep sleep to recover every night, we need to have a calm environment in which to recharge. And our home is that.'

Caitlin and Samuel's home is an ideal space to test out design ideas and allow their creativity to flourish. Their interior spaces not only feature tiles from their business, Popham Design, but many flea market finds from trips to Paris and beyond.

Caitlin & Samuel Dowe-Sandes

Q / A

What attracted you to this home?
It was a fun old place in the centre of the new town, built in the 1950s of Gueliz stone, with a small garden and room for a plunge pool. The house required a big renovation but the project was right up our alley.

What changes did you make?
We didn't change the actual footprint of the house, but everything else was fair game. We knocked down a wall between two small bedrooms to make a master bedroom, added a fireplace, converted a balcony to a guest bathroom, added a swimming pool, converted the garage to a kitchen, added and enlarged windows and French doors to the garden, and more.

What didn't you want to change?
The house has a nice layout and family feel to it. We moved to it from a one-storey bungalow, so having a second floor instantly made it feel more like a family home. Also, the downstairs has very high ceilings, which help to keep it cool in the summer, and give the house nice volumes, even though it is not a large home.

What objects hold a special meaning for you?
Artwork. Both of Samuel's parents are artists and have given us pieces over the years and we try to buy ourselves a piece of art every year on our anniversary, a tradition that started on our honeymoon in Paris. We have artwork from friends here in Marrakech, like photographer Randall Bachner.

How do you choose which items enter your home?
We tend to select things that we find beautiful or interesting, without much consideration for where they might go. Our house is decidedly eclectic, with items that remind us of our travels and different periods of our life.

How often do you edit your home and its collections?
All the time. Much to the chagrin of my husband, who is of the mind that you get it right and leave it that way. For me, rearranging furniture is the easiest inexpensive way to re-decorate. We do like to find something special on our travels, so we have evolving collections of things.

How has your style evolved over the years?
What has stayed consistent?
When we moved to Morocco, we sold our house in LA and put all of our belongings into storage. And everything is still there apart from a few pieces of art that we've liberated over the years. That means the items we have now reflect the choices of the past eleven years, influenced by our pocketbook, our travels and the design inspirations and prototype opportunities here in Marrakech. We are ten years older and the way we live has changed as well. When we first arrived in Marrakech, we were delighted with all things Moroccan – we bought pouffes, and made built-in banquettes with kilim pillows, we had lanterns everywhere and Moroccan touches like moucharabié headboards. Now, we have lived here long enough that we've circled back to our roots a bit and while the Moroccan influence remains strong, especially in our sense of layering patterns, we're back to a home that is more international, with pieces from flea markets, furniture and light fixtures we've shipped down from Europe and items we've had made here.

Which materials are important to you?
Apart from concrete! We love brass, wood, leather. Natural materials. Things that can be oiled and waxed and scarred even, that acquire a patina with age.

What gets priority in your home?
Besides the people in it – good lighting and the best tool for learning and entertainment, books, are essential in our home.

What's your favourite space?
Our bedroom. It gets a wonderful cross breeze, we look out at a stand of bamboo and there's just enough pattern play, but in an edited palette, to keep things interesting. And the light is wonderful.

When are you happy at home?
At the end of the day when I've accomplished a project or two, cooked something nice and the house is clean.

PRIORITIES

We cannot make a home without time or money. And sometimes these factors can seem insurmountable. The cost of living keeps on rising, and our finances are being stretched in an increasing number of directions. However, we are all in a position to create a beautiful home today.

We can figure out how to work around finances and time restrictions when we consider our values. They can guide our decisions on what matters most. Do we want to prioritise location or space? An old home or new build? A place we can modify or somewhere that requires little upkeep? And it's worth remembering that few of us live in our homes for a lifetime. The place we call home today may be someone else's place in five years' time.

How we create our home can resolve many of our issues over money. It's possible to design a modest shell – rather than one with expensive details and finishes – that can be easily adapted to our changing needs over the years. We can also choose to build simply and sustainably. Significant savings can be made when we visit salvage yards and buy from auction houses and second-hand sites. We can make improvements slowly over the years too. While most homes benefit from a fresh coat of paint, we don't always have to make expensive structural changes.

When we manage our priorities we can also find more time to create a home. After all, it is not lost but just spent elsewhere.

'Your vision of where or who you want to be is the greatest asset you have.'

Paul Arden

Manage priorities

How do we spend our time? Are we placing our most important tasks first? The ones that matter the most to our happiness and sense of wellbeing? Time is often cited as one of the biggest reasons that people don't make changes in their lives. However, are we really saying something is not a priority? After all, we can make time for shopping, yoga and hair appointments but not the place where we rest, relax, restore and celebrate. We can spend endless hours online but struggle to dedicate enough time to making the most of our life in the real world. How do we get back to what matters most?

Evaluation

When we consider what we value, we can design a life to complement these values. This process begins when we compare how we currently fill our days with how we would prefer to spend our time. Maybe we want to spend less time tidying, cleaning and organising our home. Perhaps, carve out a space for down time. Or we would like to entertain more. It is possible to create spaces that encourage behavioural change. By eliminating the non-essentials from our life, we can focus on what really matters. We don't have to say yes to every opportunity. Only what is really important for right now.

Money

How we spend our money speaks of our values. When it comes to our home, what do we want to prioritise? Some people choose an expensive television or coffee machine over a sofa or rug. Others buy second-hand furniture so they can invest in art. And there are those who buy high-quality furniture but wait until they can afford it and buy one piece at a time. When we are aware of the decisions we make, we can make adjustments to how we spend our money – even if it's for a period of time. We all have to make compromises but with a plan and some time we can reach tangible goals.

Perspective

It is easy to believe a sack of gold will solve all of our problems. But money can only purchase goods and services. It doesn't buy self-satisfaction – that comes from doing the work. It doesn't buy self-worth – that comes from knowing we have done the right thing. And, of course, money can't buy love – that comes from creating intimacy. Other things money can't buy: health, happiness, family, friendship, knowledge, talent, manners, respect, content children, common sense, integrity, trust, patience, time, wisdom, youth, justice, and a happy home.

Marjolein Delhaas

ROTTERDAM, NETHERLANDS

'In the Netherlands we have a special word for when an atmosphere or setting is relaxed, and you are having a good time alone or with other people. The word is *gezellig*. Apparently, there isn't an English translation but I think it comes close to the word cosy. For me, a part of *gezellig* is being able to feel at ease in a place or surrounding. Totally relaxed, at home. In our house this is the major goal. Making ourselves and the people that enter our place feel welcome and relaxed. We love to gather with family and friends, having dinners, enjoying wine, having a laugh or a good talk, but most importantly to be ourselves. *Gezelligheid* is in small things but the environment is the canvas.'

DUTCH DESIGNER MARJOLEIN DELHAAS is happiest at home when there is balance. 'I hate when a house is ordered like a museum, it should look like it is in use,' she says. 'Of course, I get crazy when the house is upside down, which happens eventually or even on a daily basis.' However, she enjoys watching stacks of objects accumulate – brought-home drawings, magazines, mail, newspapers, boxes of toys or even a school bag across the hall. 'Once in a while the piles get too high and need to be tightened up, but it is like going to the hairdresser – it looks much better a couple of days after cleaning,' she says. 'When you see again the tokens of daily life.'

The home that she has created with her husband, Tomislav, and their two young boys, Naum, five, and Filip, three, celebrates both simplicity and vitality. The 1903 property in Rotterdam had been renovated when the couple discovered it about seven years ago. At the time, they had been living in a top-floor single-storey apartment so their current two-storey home with a ground-floor living area and a garden was quite a departure. But it appealed to their plans to start a family, and both areas are now in constant use by their busy boys.

In a part of the world where distances are measured by how long it takes to cycle somewhere, the building is perfectly positioned too. It's only a five-minute ride to the city centre where Marjolein has a studio, and a similar distance to a nearby lake where Tomislav works. The family enjoys visiting the surrounding forest, which spans ten kilometres, and Filip attends daycare at a place in the woods.

While there are some things Marjolein would change about the home if she owned it, she's content to focus on hunting down vintage design classics. 'Although I love to search for beautiful, special items, I don't attach too much significance to things,' she says. 'I think that it is the story behind an object that gives it more value. The way you got it, found it or purchased it.' One such piece is the pendant that she inherited from her grandparents, which hangs above the dining table. In the same space are Castelli dining chairs, another of her finds, which she was drawn to for their minimal design and comfort. 'That goes for everything that comes into the house,' she says. 'It needs to be comfortable and functioning, and add something to our daily life.'

Marjolein is content to allow her home to evolve over the years though. 'Only then can you create a kind of soul,' she says. In the meantime, she enjoys rearranging her home to suit their changing needs, especially as the boys are still at an age when a home goes through many transitions. 'I want to bring the best out of the available spaces,' she says. 'And I like to see how our home grows in the different phases of our lives.'

TIME AND PLACE
IN NORDIC CUISINE
René Redzepi

PHAIDON

While Marjolein lives in a rental, she has made simple yet effective modifications to her home, such as the addition of industrial pendants. Also, mixing vintage finds into her pared-back space adds just enough interest without it feeling cluttered.

Marjolein Delhaas

How do you choose which items enter your home?
I love to search for vintage classics. I just got lucky and found a sixty-year-old FB18 Scissor chair by Jan van Grunsven for the Dutch label Pastoe. I can't wait to sand it and then hand it over to be refurnished. There are so many good vintage pieces that have unbeatable comfort and function. Like the small Gispen chair we have in our living room.

How often do you edit your home and its collections?
Right now we are in the middle of finding a new bed for the youngest one. It was very hard finding our first son a nice, good bed. But when we found it – a Piet Hein Eek Crisis bed – it was such a joy and still is. It is simple but beautiful. You should see how beautifully the mattress bottom has been made. I don't like having lots of stuff. I am not a collector in the sense that I do not need to hold on to many things. I do not fancy too much decoration. I can easily get rid of things that are in my way. You don't need many things to create a great space and atmosphere or have a good time. It is more what you choose and how you live in it. Full closets, every inch used, creates a certain chaos in my head. So, I have a rule: I try to only buy something new if it replaces something, if it is really an addition to the way we live or if it is a storage item. Of course, there are exceptions to that rule, but it does help prevent me making worthless impulse purchases.

What's involved in the process?
It is almost like in my work, I will do thorough research before finally deciding on something and buying it.

How has your style evolved over the years?
Overall it has stayed the same, it's just that now I have some more money to spend and realise it's worth buying something you really like, especially when you love to spend time in your home.

Which materials are important to you?
Quality, comfortable and natural materials. I love materials such as wood, steel, concrete, wool, plain cotton, linen.

How do you like to use colour in your home?
My canvas is mostly minimalistic, lots of white and neutral tones as I love to let our daily life bring the colour and flavour to it. Kids running around, colourful toys, stacks of magazines, drawings on the cupboard or kitchen door, flowers and plants. Or just a bunch of clothes on the floor. Fresh fruit, vegetables and bread in the kitchen, the smell of cooking and, of course, having the right light – burning many, many candles – and playing music.

What gets priority in your home?
Fresh flowers, the garden, (roughly) made beds, open curtains. And in my dreams … no washing.

What's your favourite space?
It depends on my mood. In summer, our garden, in the morning our kitchen, in the afternoon our living room and on summer evenings I love to be in the bedroom early, reading a book on our bed or doing some yoga practice. The evenings in summer are long and light, the light in the back of the house is so good. We spend much time at the dinner table, playing games, eating, drinking or just talking. In winter, I love our living room, as the rest of the house gets more cold. With lots of lit candles everywhere, pillows and blankets on the sofa.

What do you think makes a welcoming home?
The people living in it.

'The wisdom of
life consists in the
elimination of
non-essentials.'

Lin Yutang

two

LIVE

LIVING

BEAUTY

SENSE

LIVE

There can be a tendency to consider homes as objects, such as cars or computers. They are assigned a checklist of parts and expected to be assembled in the way of machines. But homes can't be created with spreadsheets or formulas. And beware of what's online, especially image libraries. ———— Homes must not start with the end in mind. They need to begin with our story. To unearth a home, we have to dig deep – to understand ourselves as well as others who live there, how a space will be used, and how it will be felt. The focus of home design needs to shift from the surface to the sensory. We stimulate our senses every time we enter a space. Our choice of materials plays a significant role in the experience of our home, and the telling of our story. That's when a home becomes beautiful – when it touches on a truth. That's when we want to linger in a space – when we feel a deeper narrative at play. It creates intrigue. ———— In the words of John Keats, 'Beauty is truth, truth beauty.' Let's express our truth. Because we enhance our lives when we create wholehearted homes.

'Beauty is nothing other than the promise of happiness.'
Stendahl

LIVING

The traditional way to design a house is from the outside in – starting with the walls and finding ways to fill the structure from a checklist of rooms, furniture and collections. The humanist approach puts a person at the heart of a space. As designer Ilse Crawford says, we must ask the big questions first. What does our home mean to us? How do we want to feel in it? What do we value? It's an inside-out approach that considers how we engage with and experience a space. As Crawford says, a home should meet human needs and desires, not intellectual ideas and concepts. It's also not a list of objects to buy. Instead, the interior reflects what we value in life.

This approach overlaps with the Danish concept of *hygge*, which is often translated as cosiness but extends to how the Danes create a general sense of wellbeing. The Dutch have a similar word, *gezellig*, which is about feeling welcome and relaxed in a space. And the Germans have *gemütlichkeit,* deriving from the word *gemüt*, relating to the heart, mind, temper and feeling. Similar words exist in Bulgarian, Russian, Turkish and Thai. The Japanese concept of *wabi-sabi*, finding beauty in imperfection, is a step removed from the Northern European take on environment, but it does celebrate the human element in life. These ideas focus on how we feel at home and have been embraced in recent years as part of our continual search for happiness. Interestingly, Denmark is often ranked as one of the happiest nations in the world.

But are these ideas transferable? Is there some universality to what we value? Or do we all need to work out our individual needs? And how does it all relate to our home life?

'Who looks outside, dreams; who looks inside, awakes.'

Carl Jung

Elevate function

While there are obvious commonalities to our basic needs and desires, homes cannot be designed with a one-size-fits-all approach. We need to integrate the way we live into our spaces. Homes should enhance our everyday – through the way they function and feel.

Personalisation

Happiness at home comes in many hues. What's important to us about our home? Do we value privacy? Or need a space to retreat? Is entertaining important? Which areas currently get congested? Which are hardly used? These questions need to come before creating concepts or specifying products.

Rituals

We all have different daily rituals too, and our homes need to accommodate them. Do we enjoy cooking and creating an array of dishes? If so, we should ensure there is enough bench space to accommodate a line-up of plates. Do we spend time working at home? Then an office or study away from the noise of the kitchen and living areas might be preferable. Each person and their needs should be taken into consideration, with an honest assessment of how we use a space, as well as factoring in how it relates to the rest of the home.

Reality

Homes function well when we are realistic about human traits. Are we neat or messy? A glance around right now will provide the answer. A home has to absorb our habits and behavioural patterns. When we think through our daily movements we can see where our spaces inhibit function or pleasure. Do cups and plates tend to congregate around the sink? Do clothes pile up on the bedroom floor? Where do we put our shoes when we enter the house? We can use this knowledge to make decisions that will make our home more liveable.

Movement

Homes provide an opportunity to bring pleasure at every turn and enhance our feelings of wellbeing. When we design a space we need to envisage life moving through it. We can start at the entrance and move through and around rooms. And consider spaces in relation to our bodies – do we want to feel enveloped in a space or small against a soaring ceiling and expansive views? Factor in preferences too – do we want a luxurious bathing experience or a separate laundry? And when there are multiple people in the house, how will everyone move through spaces in relation to each other? There are areas best suited to communal living, and other zones where we want to avoid bottlenecks. Private spaces where we can reconnect with ourselves are important too.

Emotion

When design blends intelligence and emotion, it enhances our lives. A large dining table that seats many guests feels warm and welcoming. A sofa with a relaxed and random arrangement of feather-filled cushions is a seat we want to sink into. And a console with a welcoming arrangement – flowers, perhaps – near a front door feels inviting. A space enhances our lives when it has purpose and appeals to our senses.

Claire Delmar

'Home is about family, friends and re-energising. It's also about a sense of security and a place I feel creative, as well as calm. It's somewhere I feel proud to be an Australian and to have the opportunity to live in the outdoors and watch the kids play safely in the yard. It's about cooking and learning together as a family and having friends over for games, drinks and laughs. It's a place to potter and spend time on the weekends away from the hustle and bustle of the outside world. It's a place to escape and read. The home is everything to me as a mother, wife, stylist and passionate cook. It encapsulates the entirety of what makes me who I am and gives me a purpose, as well as – fortunately – a career that is forever changing but always challenging and inspiring.'

STYLIST CLAIRE DELMAR ENJOYS immersing herself in a project. 'Creating spaces is what I do so I would never feel comfortable in a home that had already been designed and stamped with someone else's personality,' she says. It was inevitable then when she and her husband, James, were looking to buy a house for their young family in 2012, that it would be somewhere that required work.

While Claire was confident and capable of making improvements, she was mindful to seek out the inherent features in a home that often cannot be changed. 'What I noticed when I first entered the house was the light that filled the internal space and an essential feeling of privacy,' she says. The garden aspect was also a drawcard for Claire who often works from home.

The couple wanted to make the most of the downstairs living area, and it was the first place they tackled. Removing a wall from the kitchen helped to extend the space and new flooring tied the rooms together. A couple of years later they opened up the back of the house, extended the deck and installed bi-fold doors to create a large indoor and outdoor room.

At the same time, the couple were raising young children, son Leo, eight, and daughter Willow, two. And while Claire's home showcases a stylist's eye and deft touch, she doesn't labour over the space. 'I must say I wish I had more time to style my own space but as it's my day job, I tend to come home, switch off and don't think too

much about it,' she says. However, Claire is still happy with the design and palette of the initial renovation.

'I tend to feel an instant love for something that doesn't fade and I know it has to come home with me,' she says. 'Because I am flooded with product on a daily basis, it doesn't happen very often. You tend to be numbed by the overload of beauty.'

Claire has cultivated strong instincts when it comes to making decisions for her home. 'Having styled for so many years, editing my space tends to stem from a feeling, rather than a process,' she says. 'Knowing there's no right or wrong, my approach is individual and personal, and it depends on what my eye is drawn to and engaged by. Changes have to make me feel good and are dependent on the palette I find myself drawn to, along with my mood, or the season.'

Underpinning her aesthetic is a huge appreciation for twentieth-century design. 'A love for architecture came at a very early age whilst studying the Bauhaus school of thought, and it was this interest that fuelled the fire within,' she says. 'Modernism and iconic furniture inspired my design principles and it's the art of layering within this pared-back space of simple materials, that defines the design.'

Claire's home is for living though. She loves nothing more than to cook for friends and family. 'Entertaining is a passion and the kitchen is where I switch off from the day and create in a new way,' she says.

Claire Delmar

Claire has a passion for ceramics
and has slowly added to her collection
over the years. In the kitchen her
pieces are showcased against waxed
compressed cement.

Claire Delmar

Why did you move to this area?
We knew the area well from having walked our first child countless times in the early hours of the morning through Centennial Park to the local coffee shop down the lane. It was always a goal to be close to both Centennial Park and the eastern beaches.

What attracted you to this home?
I was immediately attracted to the house's sense of space and its potential.

What didn't you want to change?
We would never want to change the gorgeous original windows in the living room. And although we both prefer a box design, we didn't want to modify too much of the 'Cape Cod' roof before we decided whether we were going to add a new extension and remove the point, or extend into the ceiling and expose the beams.

How does your home make you feel?
There's almost nothing more I'd rather do than to 'potter' around spaces and the house allows me to do that perfectly.

What objects hold a special meaning for you?
My ceramics bring me so much joy. I'm gathering quite a collection now and love to source one-off, handmade pieces from artists that each tell a story. There is also a special place in my heart for Claire Goddard's paper spoons. My husband gave them to me on our first 'paper' anniversary when we were living in the UK. It is important for me to be surrounded by objects that are associated with memories of special times.

How do you choose which items enter your home?
As I'm getting older I am choosing quality over quantity, and my choices focus on items that follow good design principles.

How often do you edit your home and its collections?
As a school student, I used to constantly edit my room as a form of procrastination – anything but study. But I do think my natural tendency to be highly organised has helped me in my career. I try to edit my props every few months but within the house the special personal collections rarely get edited. Some occasionally get moved, similarly to a visual gallery, but rarely do they get cut from the scene. Because of my personal style every item works together. I particularly love to see how pieces tell a different story within a new space or position, or when coupled with different items.

How has your style evolved over the years?
What has stayed consistent?
My style has become more refined with time and exposure, along with the accumulation of knowledge from diverse shoots and jobs. Although I have found a style I love, pared-back simplicity has remained pivotal.

Which materials are important to you?
I've always been drawn to cement, wood and anything textured.

When are you happy at home?
I'm happiest when my home is being shared with others, and of course when it's clean and neat and the kids have picked up their toys.

'A home's personality stems from individual items that can't be sourced in a day but are instead curated over the years, each telling a story about the people inside. Layers are what creates a home and an interest to an outsider's eye.'

Claire

Paul & Sophie Yanacopoulos-Gross

NEW YORK, USA

'Home is your temple, your root, your anchor, your territory, your protection, your expression. Your home is an extension of your body and of your spirit. If you are connected to your home then you are connected to yourself. It is the container of our possessions and memories. It is our refuge. It is the place of reunion and of our private sharing. It is the place of regeneration, of inspiration. It is the nest of the family. Loving your home means loving yourself.'

WHEN YOU'RE A FOREIGNER in a new place you have to create your own environment, you have to create your own shell,' says Sophie Yanacopoulos-Gross, a designer and shop owner. It's an experience that's still relatively fresh in her mind after moving from the Swiss countryside to the urban streets of New York with her husband and business partner Paul, and their children, Theodore, eighteen, and Athéna, fourteen, as well as dog Atlas.

'We have undergone massive change, leaving space and peace behind for the stimulation of gritty city life,' Paul says. 'NYC is an exhausting mess of a place. Despite this, it is endlessly invigorating and inspiring. Home recharges the batteries.'

The family made the move at the end of 2016 and soon found an historic home in Brooklyn Heights that was within walking distance of their furniture and homewares store, HomeStories. 'We fell in love with the charm and the soul of the place,' Sophie says. 'It's important to have an environment that suits your spirit when your profession is linked to interiors.'

While the home is a rental they have been keen to embrace the charm of the building, and work in the collection of furniture and decorative objects that has been part of their lives for many years. 'We have changed furniture occasionally but never style,' Sophie says. 'We have had the same taste and palette for twenty years, at least.' The constant threads have been simplicity and quality, as well as natural materials such as wood, linen and cotton.

It's an approach that Sophie learnt in part from her Swedish mother. 'She would make triviality poetic,' she says. 'There are no minor or major objects. You can create beauty with anything. When I shop, for example, I want the food to have aesthetic qualities. I'm not going to buy packaging that's horrible if I can avoid it.' However, she says Paul is less inconvenienced by the detritus of day-to-day living but enjoys putting decorative ideas into play. Together they have created harmony in their home and a feeling of permanence even though they are still adjusting to life in New York.

The living room is where the family comes together. It has become a place for relaxing, listening, talking, resting and watching, Paul says. It reflects the shift in their family dynamic as their children are on the cusp of independence and they are all embracing a new frontier in a foreign land. 'We are very grateful to be able to enjoy this magical place in the heart of Brooklyn Heights,' Sophie says.

'I need to surround myself with poetry – I need poetry all the time.'

Sophie

Paul & Sophie Yanacopoulos-Gross

Paul & Sophie Yanacopoulos-Gross

Paul & Sophie Yanacopoulos-Gross

Paul & Sophie Yanacopoulos-Gross

Why did you move here?
Paul (P): It's a dream location. For us, it's one of the top three streets anywhere in NYC. You can open the windows at night and wake to birds chirping. A town house in the country.

What attracted you to this home?
P: The farmhouse in France charm. The rarity of finding a home that has not been renovated. It's all the more honest because of its imperfections.

Sophie (S): You cannot be happy in an environment that you cannot relate to. It is fundamental to have a peaceful relationship with your interior.

What didn't you want to change?
P: The imperfections and there are many.

S: We feel it is so important to keep the spirit of this place. One can always make changes but when you rent a place it invites you to adapt, which can lead to a lot of possibilities.

How does your home make you feel?
P: Warm, protected, at peace. We have recently moved from Europe and have undergone massive change.

S: Our home has a very comforting soul. It has a warmth and a cosiness that is very inviting. I am as happy alone or with family and friends. I have also re-discovered the joy of gardening.

What objects hold a special meaning for you?
P: All objects hold a meaning. Each interacts, each has a certain specific beauty.

S: We are big object collectors. We cannot help but buy some or recuperate unsold ones. Therefore, we are surrounded by multiple periods, old and new, valuable and poor, chosen or unchosen.

How do you choose which items enter your home?
P: As we have a shop, objects come and go. We test everything we sell. Most of the furniture is designed by us. However, no object has arrived in our household by accident. All are chosen with care and love and all have special meaning to us.

S: Natural woods, natural linens, painted wood, white covers, natural carpets and rugs, baskets, art pieces, photography, simple kitchenware, simple white sheets and bath linen, curiosities, books, art books, music equipment.

How often do you edit your home and its collections?
P: Continuously. It is a joyful yet endless process.

What's involved in the process?
P: Our home is a laboratory to experiment. We are currently prototyping our first light and are trying out linen shades and proportions. The living room has, for the first time in our family life, become a place for gathering, talking, resting and watching. This is new for us as the kitchen has always been the centre of operations.

How has your style evolved over the years?
P: Change is fundamental to our evolution. Without it we stagnate.

S: We have evolved but our style has remained the same. Simplicity and quality.

What gets priority in your home?
P: Family time.

S: Light. When you have the right light, you have the right feel. Having a clean space and clean windows is the fundamental base. Letting natural light enter the space.

What's your favourite space?
P: For the first time ever, the living room.

S: Our bedroom. It is a very majestic space and its proportions are amazing. It used to be a living room on the second floor and has three windows reflecting the garden. So the natural imposed colour is a very tender green. It is the place I regenerate myself and share with my other half.

When are you happy at home?
P: In this home, always. Our sleep patterns are very different here. We have a very long and deep sleep.

S: I am very happy when we enjoy the fireplace with friends and family. Or a dinner in the garden. I also very much enjoy the quietness of early mornings when the family sleeps.

What do you think makes a welcoming home?
P: The light, the warmth of material, but none matter without a joyous household.

S: The atmosphere. If you walk into a loved home you will feel an atmosphere that is welcoming.

BEAUTY

Beautiful homes are something to behold. But they are also a matter of perception. If a space makes us happy, does it matter what others think? Too much focus on beauty can distract from many more worthy endeavours, yet its pursuit is one of the defining characteristics of humankind. It underpins the history of art and literature, and is evident in science and maths too. Why? 'A feeling of beauty is a sign that we have come upon a material articulation of certain of our ideas of a good life,' wrote philosopher Alain de Botton in *The Architecture of Happiness*.

Beauty provides us with an alternative to its opposites – ugliness, crudeness, inelegance. Perhaps even chaos. And we tend to not want those elements in our lives. There's a reason why most Brutalist buildings were designed for institutions rather than homes.

There are also times when we need an antidote or respite from our day-to-day existence. What we require from our surroundings can be a reaction to the age we're living in. During the nineteenth century's industrial revolution, artworks featuring bucolic scenes became a balm to the increasing mechanisation of the world. Similarly, now in this time of great technological advance, there is a boom in the artisanal and the handmade. There are many books and websites dedicated to rustic cabins and nature-based lifestyles. Popular photographic artworks feature oceanscapes and tropical scenes. We crave what is just beyond our reach.

However, sometimes we cannot see that we already live amongst beauty. The busyness of our lives obscures it. But our homes are filled with beauty – light, shadows, forms, sometimes even an outlook. We just need to give ourselves the time and space to appreciate everyday beauty. And our homes can benefit from nature's order – creating beauty with purpose.

'Pare down to the essence but don't remove the poetry.'

Leonard Koren

Create true beauty

Can a space possess beauty and not feel like a home? There are certainly many that photograph strikingly but have no soul. Others create a statement but provide little comfort. A home's beauty should be more than skin deep. It needs to be authentic and possess an inner confidence and truth rather than mere show and bravado.

When a room has balance and harmony, we don't feel threatened. Instead we are at ease and engage with the choices on display. It doesn't matter what visual story is being told, which materials have been used, or whether the room is layered or pared back, we appreciate beauty when it is created with integrity. These are the spaces where we want to be.

Composition

When we create spaces, we should consider the balance of a room. It is often overlooked. But the space between objects is just as important as the objects themselves. It's something photographers use in the composition of an image. They seek to create negative space so the eye has time to focus on what's within the frame. Another technique is to divide images into thirds and weight them top or bottom heavy depending on the subject. We also need to compose our spaces carefully to create harmony. Homes that get the balance right with objects within a space are appealing. A sofa that's too large for a room can look clumsy and feel overwhelming. A dining table that's squeezed into a space doesn't feel welcoming. And a rug that's too small can feel miserly – balance isn't always about making objects smaller in relation to their surrounds. Even within our homes, it's true that the whole is greater than the sum of its parts. How pieces work together determines if a room feels harmonious and inviting. Rooms benefit from repetition to create rhythm and negative space to facilitate flow. We need to be mindful of how rooms relate to adjoining spaces too. We can create a sense of connection through colour or material choices while allowing each zone to stand alone.

Heart

Every room can benefit from something special at its heart – usually a key piece of furniture that provides beauty and purpose. This can be an everyday essential such as a sofa, dining table or bed. But sometimes artworks, mirrors or architectural elements can be the engaging heart. These items are often viewed from the entrance to the room and are framed with layers of interest from other elements such as rugs and lamps. These heartfelt feature pieces also set the tone. Do we want to create a grand statement or a space that's calm and serene?

Imagination

There are times when bare walls provide relief for the eyes. But when every wall is empty, and furniture lacks scale, a space can feel barren. However, there are many ways to fill wall spaces, and plenty of alternatives to art canvases. We can consider sculptural pieces foraged from nature, vintage clothes to hang, lighting with a strong sense of form or scale, or whatever else feels authentic to our story.

Caroline Carter

MELBOURNE, AUSTRALIA

'To me, home is a feeling. Without love it is just a house. I am lucky to live here, surrounded by my loved ones and beautiful things. It is a happy and safe place. And while it is also noisy and chaotic, it's where I can nurture, collect and create.'

HISTORY WEAVES ITS WAY through the home of Caroline Carter in many ways. While she lives in an unassuming suburban brick house from the 1970s on the outskirts of Melbourne, it holds many special memories. The house belonged to her grandma and was where Caroline spent a lot of her childhood. She and her husband, Darren, bought the three-bedroom house almost a decade ago with the view to create their own family home for children Jett, twelve, and Lila, five, after Caroline's grandma passed away. 'The house has such a good position with beautiful mountain views,' she says. 'And, of course, very fond memories for me.'

In a time when the size of family homes has increased a great deal, Caroline was attracted to the intimacy of the place. 'I really love small, simple houses,' she says. And the smaller home meant that the couple could live within their means too. They had a tight budget and didn't want to stretch to structural changes. However, everything else was replaced – from windows and doors to carpets and gutters. Walls were rendered, floorboards polished and roof tiles painted. 'I just wanted a really simple white classic look that would work with any interior decoration,' she says.

Caroline's love of vintage pieces is one of the defining features of the home. 'I've always loved to collect, craft and decorate,' she says. About fifteen years ago Caroline started collecting vintage pieces seriously when she had her own homewares shop. 'My taste has changed since then but my love of vintage hasn't,' she says. 'These days I look for impact. I don't have a huge budget and actually fall in love with what people would consider junk. I enjoy making something from nothing. And I like to mix those pieces in with a few key investment pieces.'

Given the size of her collection, editing it regularly is essential. 'I might find one new piece that will set the ball rolling,' Caroline says. 'I rarely go looking for anything. If it finds me it comes home and I make it work somehow. Even if it means changing a room completely.'

Caroline jokes that her family thinks she's crazy. A common question is, 'You want to do what?' But they are used to her rearranging the home, and expeditions to vintage shops, which they also enjoy. 'The children ask me if we can go to "The French Shop"', she says, 'which is their name for any vintage shop.'

Patience is key for Caroline when it comes to adding layers to her home. The standing lamp in her living room was purchased from a dealer in France. 'I saved and saved for this piece,' she says. And she's content to live with Ikea sofas until she can find her dream replacements, even though she's not sure what they are yet. 'I like to take my time and be sure,' she says. 'I'm really happy with what we have and I'm patient.'

The home's statement pieces, including the lockers and the tureen collection, are Caroline's favourites. 'I love them and appreciate them so much because I saved so hard for them,' she says.

Caroline Carter

How does your home make you feel?
So many things! It makes me feel safe and happy. I love the monochrome palette; I find it very calming.

What attracted you to this home?
It is in a lovely neighbourhood and it was my grandparents' home so has a beautiful feeling as well. I grew up coming here so knew the house and the garden.

What didn't you want to change?
The layout and size. I really love small, simple houses.

What objects hold a special meaning for you?
I love everything in the house but my favourite pieces are my 'statement' pieces, like the lockers, portraits and my tureen collection. All French.

How do you choose which items enter your home?
Colour! I also have to love it and it must be useful as well. I like to buy simple statement pieces. I'm happy to live with less but what I have has to make a big impact. I find collections work really well as quite often you can buy a whole lot of one thing and display them for impact.

How often do you edit your home and its collections?
All the time. Certain things always stay but I'm always tweaking the edges.

What's involved in the process?
There isn't a process as such. I may find something new that needs to come home, quite often this upsets the balance I have, so something needs to go. Thus it begins.

How has your style evolved over the years?
It has simplified. Less is more.

What has stayed consistent?
My love of vintage.

Which materials are important to you?
I like a mix of industrial, rustic and natural elements but I'm also attracted to modern, simple design. The materials need to be practical and easy to care for and keep clean with children. They need to improve with extra dents and scratches.

What gets priority in your home?
I always feel happy when everything is in place, so cleaning and tidying, definitely.

What's your favourite space?
The dining area with the crates and my big chalkboard and plaster sculpture.

When are you happy at home?
I'm happy when I'm cooking, creating and decorating.

What makes a welcoming home?
Happiness.

'It stimulates my creativity being surrounded by my favourite things.'

Caroline

Katrin Arens

BERGAMO, ITALY

'My house at the river is my home; it represents our lives – simple and sophisticated. It's a great luxury having all this space without anybody living close by. We have freedom to do whatever we want – throw parties, listen to loud music – without disturbing anybody around. This house gives me the feeling of home – protection and freedom. And feeling at home is where my family stays, where we spend time together, which is wonderful in the old mill at the river.'

AN IMPERFECT HOUSE GIVES the gift of freedom, says furniture designer Katrin Arens. *'La casa mi da una grande libertà,'* she says. 'Free to create and free to be.' It's an idea that Katrin's been able to play out in her home in a former fifteenth-century monastery – which later became a mill house – near Bergamo, in the Lombardy region of Italy.

She found the abandoned building on the banks of the river Adda about twenty years ago when she was looking for a place where she could set up an atelier and home. At the time she was also pregnant with her eldest daughter, Laura, who is now eighteen. Her younger daughter, Sofia, is eleven.

While Katrin studied economics and graphic design in Germany, where she was born and raised, she moved to Italy after winning a scholarship at the Academy of Arts in Bergamo. In 1996 Katrin started designing furniture from recycled materials, with a focus on pieces that were perceived to have no value, such as wood used for scaffolding. Her business continues to make furniture and has expanded to include kitchen designs, which are sent all over the world.

While the atelier started on the ground floor of the house, it has since been relocated to a nearby village. And the building, which was used as a mill house until 1960, is no longer the family's primary home. Instead they are based in town during the week to be close to school, friends and sports commitments. However, they return on weekends and school holidays. It still functions as their main home in many ways. It's where Katrin enjoys cooking and entertaining, and the girls can enjoy each other's company. 'We spend a lot of time in the kitchen,' she says. 'It's our living room.'

From the kitchen window the mountain Resegone is visible in the distance, and below is the River Adda. 'The position of the house is perfect,' Katrin says. It was one of the attractions of the building, as well as the light and the big rooms.

However, the site had been abandoned for about ten years before they moved in. There was no electricity, hot water or heating. Windows were broken and swallows had built nests in the ceiling. While they cleaned out the residence and installed basic necessities, Katrin wanted to keep the place as close to its origins as possible. 'No strange materials or big changes,' she says.

Since the initial improvements, the building has stayed mostly the same over the past twenty years. Most of the furniture is Katrin's design. And there are a few other pieces that the family has collected on their travels. The main changes have been to accommodate the needs of the girls, who have grown up in the house. Katrin is happiest when they are all together.

Katrin maintained the existing structure of her home but freshened it up with paint. Furniture has been kept to a minimum and includes heirloom pieces, such as the wardrobe in her bedroom.

Q / A

When and why did you move here?
We moved into the house in 1998. Laura was born here. I was looking for a place where I could live and work, so I had my furniture production in the rooms below.

What changes did you make?
The house was abandoned for about ten years before we moved in. There were no basic amenities and birds flying in and out.

What didn't you want to change?
I wanted to keep its original condition authentic, but with just a bit more comfort, like hot water, electricity and heating.

What objects hold a special meaning for you?
We love travelling to different countries and we are fascinated about other cultures so we always bring some objects back with us to the house.

How do you choose which items enter your home?
They have to be authentic and they have to respect my philosophy. They have to tell a story or mean something to me, such as remembering a voyage.

How often do you edit your home and its collections?
I only changed and rearranged the house when it was necessary with my kids. Most of the house remains the way it is. I only add some objects after coming back from a voyage, sometimes only a few things such as a plate or little stool.

How has your style evolved over the years?
My furniture production is the same since 1996, the only evolution is that from the production of single pieces, now we mostly do interior projects, especially kitchens. But the style is the same, always working with simple and 'poor' materials, keeping its originality – seeing where it comes from. My home in Germany where I grew up was filled with antique furniture, mostly Biedermeier and Jugendstil. My mom was a fan of this period mixed with modern pieces. I started to be interested in 'old' furniture when I was a kid in the 1970s when people threw away a lot of old furniture. In Germany they used to have

Sperrmuell once a month – people put everything out on the streets in front of their house and big trash-vans came early in the morning picking up everything to throw it away. At night, people were looking with a torch collecting things, such as chairs, etc. I remember I was so fascinated by what other peopler threw away – sometimes incredible beautiful things.

Which materials are important to you?
Natural wood and anything that keeps the house in its original state.

What gets priority in your home?
I like to have natural colours and white in the house – and allow objects to introduce colour. I need to feel relaxed at home.

When are you happy at home?
When we are together with all the family and friends at home. We celebrate a lot of parties with our friends at home or simply have lunch or dinner with our friends in summer in the garden. The rest of the year in our big kitchen. We always celebrate Christmas in the house with a big tree at the end of the long entrance. In summer we all go swimming in the river.

What do you think makes a welcoming home?
An open house where all of our beloved family and friends are always welcome, especially when they come unexpectedly.

We have a special white linen tablecloth which is ten metres long that we use for our special dinners and anniversaries and we stitch all the dates and names in this tablecloth and I share it with my friend Doris Zehr who lives in a beautiful renaissance castle in Germany.

For the tableware I use my white tableware that I produce in Puglia, because food brings the colour, mixed with different old glasses from my family or flea markets. Also, I give the house to artists when I'm on vacation, so they work there and as an exchange they leave a piece of their work.

SENSE

We are at an interesting junction in this age of information. We are living in a time of intangibles. We communicate without speaking. Shop without stepping in-store. Trade without touching money. Friendships are forged on our devices, children's lives are shared in little virtual squares and love is found online. Never before have we been so removed from the touchstones of day-to-day living. And yet the more detached we are from the physical, the more we crave it.

Handmade is no longer a pejorative term. It is something we seek. Whole industries are thriving on the back of artisanal products and services, and the use of 'honest' materials. We enjoy feeling connected to the people who make our goods, and value human creation in perfectly imperfect pieces. The more our world is automated, the more we want to embrace nature too.

One manifestation of this movement is our renewed interest in outdoor living and cabin-style homes. Timber cladding and rough-sawn timber are being incorporated inside homes. Increasingly we prefer to see the grain of timber on floors and furniture, rather than drowning it in layers of polyurethane or enamel. Above all others, wood is our preferred material. Architect Frank Lloyd Wright called it 'the most humanely intimate of all materials'.

But there are other materials that create intimacy too. Linen is a fabric that softens against our skin. Wool connects us to nature and timeless processes. And when we layer our homes with fabrics and textiles with a long history, we tap into a longer narrative of creativity that can enhance our sense of wellbeing.

Our homes have never been so important. They provide us with a space to create intimacy. They are where we can *feel* – tangibly and emotionally. And they are our shelter, not just from the elements but the 'noise' of the world. So when we think about what we want of our place, let's ask ourselves how we want to feel.

'The eye – it cannot choose but see; we cannot bid the ear be still;
our bodies feel, where'er they be, against or with our will.'

Wordsworth

Appeal to the senses

More than half of the brain dedicates itself to deciphering sensory information. Our bodies are made of organs that respond to stimulae. Our eyes react to light. Our skin responds to touch. Our ears hum to sound. Then there is taste and smell, as well as other more acute senses. Yet we often overlook them when making decisions in relation to our homes. But they can evoke strong feelings. Consider the sound of footsteps on solid timber floorboards versus linoleum, and how each experience makes us feel. Or our response to seeing sunlight dance along sheer curtains. Design and emotion are intricately linked.

Materials

It is well known that colour plays a huge role in our perception of a space. However, even when we are working with a neutral palette, our senses can decipher nuances in shades, tones and textures. This is true of materials too – our bodies can feel the difference between synthetic and natural fibres.

What if we embrace materials that accentuate our senses? Tiles that remind us of travelling to a far-flung destination or fabric found at a vintage market. Objects don't exist in isolation. They evoke peripheral memories – the heat of the day, smell of food, the sounds of a market. These emotional connections can enhance the everyday experience of using our home.

Timelessness

There's a reason some materials continue to be used in our homes after thousands of years. Not only are they inherently beautiful and practical, but they connect us to the history of homes and help make us feel grounded in our own. And while technology has produced materials that stain less and are more durable, the result is sometimes cold surfaces that provide little emotional connection. Because that's the point of timber and marble, both of which stain, scratch and discolour. They are the living canvas of our lives. And synthetic materials, such as plastic, no matter how well designed or engineered, rarely make us feel good.

Good sense

Sustainable choices make good sense. And while ethical and sustainable lifestyles are de rigueur in some communities, the world at large does not seem interested in taking better care of the environment. It's more than twenty-five years since global leaders met at the Rio Earth Summit yet since then our ecological footprint has grown, global populations of many fish, birds and mammals continue to decline, and greenhouse gas emissions are rising. When it comes to our homes, our first choice should always be to consider what we can re-use, repair or recycle. This approach comes with benefits. Vintage and second-hand items add character to our homes. Custom one-off solutions become part of our story too. And they make us feel good that we are not adding to the growing number of products consumed daily around the world.

Irene Mertens

AMSTERDAM, NETHERLANDS

'For me, home needs to be relaxed: no TV, natural materials, relaxing music, good food,
nice people, a lot of plants and greenery, an inspiring book and a nice chat and laugh with
the people around me – joy and creativity. The house also needs to be clean and organised.
No mess, and well kept.'

HOME IS A WAY OF LIFE for Dutch designer Irene Mertens. It is one that prioritises thoughtful choices in materials and textures. A place that both stimulates and calms the senses. The name behind the lifestyle brand that she runs with her business partner Sam IJsbrandy, Sukha, translates to mean 'joy of life'.

Irene grew up in Oss, in the south of the Netherlands, but has lived in Amsterdam for twenty-five years. She studied at the Amsterdam Fashion Institute and the Academy of Art and Design in Arnhem and worked in publishing for twelve years before starting her own business seven years ago. At first, she worked alone but now she runs it with Sam. What started as a shop in Amsterdam is now an atelier with products that sell all over the world. But this is not a story of global expansion but rather sustainable living. Good-quality and natural materials are at the heart of the story, and they are all road tested in a space that Irene calls home in the broadest sense.

About four years ago she found a former garage that she wanted to turn into a studio space for her business and a place to live with her husband, Gabriel van Beek, a recruitment consultant. 'It was a really dark space with no light,' she says. Her vision was to create an ecological home. All the walls are straw bale and the design is according to shamanistic principles. Fire is in the corner and water from the kitchen

and bathroom are positioned nearby. 'It's so the energy stream can go through,' Irene says. 'It's all done naturally, and it is better for your health.' The idea was to work in an area near the front door, live at the other end of the 35 metre-long building and keep the space open. 'We like to see the streets and the garden – and that's the idea,' Irene says.

After getting permission, the build process took about two years. Initially the plan was to keep the whole space open plan. 'When I bought the place I didn't expect to have a child so that's why we didn't build any rooms,' Irene says. However, she now has a two-year-old daughter, Juul. Window frames have helped to create partitions while still allowing light to flood through a skylight that covers most of the building. They were added during the reconstruction of the roof, which resulted in the discovery of original wooden beams hidden behind a concrete ceiling.

Despite the arduous build process, the home appears as if it has always been this way. The family moved into the completed house two years ago and continue to adapt it to their needs. 'It changes all the time because we have the space,' Irene says. 'And we make a lot ourselves.' Many of the products from the atelier make their way into the home. In some ways Irene has struck something of an ideal work-life balance, because it's all a joy.

Irene Mertens

Irene Mertens

When Irene originally rebuilt her home
it was one large open space. After the
birth of her daughter, she adapted it
to partition off the bedroom.

Irene Mertens

Q / A

What attracted you to this home?
It was a big space in the city centre; it was a garage but with a lot of potential. You hardly see places like this, with over 300 square metres.

What changes did you make?
Everything – only the four walls stayed; the rest was renovated in an ecological way. We installed water, electricity, a bathroom and a kitchen. There was nothing here.

What didn't you want to change?
The ceiling. We did a lot of reconstruction in the ceiling, renovating the wood. It was wet and dirty, but we cleaned it. The ceiling is one of the most authentic parts of the house.

How does your home make you feel?
Relaxed and calm, because of the colours and the materials like clay and wool. All neutral and organic in natural colours. There is a kind of emptiness with a warm feeling.

How often do you edit your home and its collections?
It changes all the time because we have the space. And we make a lot ourselves. We test Atelier Sukha products at home.

What objects hold a special meaning for you?
Things bought on my travels.

How do you choose which items enter your home?
Only natural ones; no plastics or metals in the house. We love to work with wood, clay, wool and cotton.

How has your style evolved over the years?
It's stayed consistent, natural and more and more pure over the years. Natural dyes and organic materials are very important.

Which materials are important to you?
Wood, wool, cotton and clay. I love different kinds of papers too.

What gets priority in your home?
A relaxing space like the couch.

What's your favourite space?
In the back near the fireplace. It is very silent.

When are you happy at home?
In the morning drinking my first coffee or late in the evening with a relaxing tea.

What do you think makes a welcoming home?
Warm materials and a good smell.

'Whatever is sought for can be caught ... whatever is neglected slips away.'

Sophocles

three

NURTURE

BELONGING

BALANCE

INGENUITY

KINDNESS

NURTURE

So much of the dialogue about homes relates to their beginning. But that's only part of the journey. ——— Homes provide the foundations for our lives and the backdrop for events that will one day become our memories. We need to create flexible spaces that can adapt to the continual shifts and changes – the unexpected house guests and big-number birthday parties we host from time to time. It helps if we are not overly precious about our spaces too. When we let go of perfection and other restrictive ways of thinking, we give ourselves the freedom to play and learn, and reduce our stress levels. And when we give, we get back more. When we open the doors to our home and break bread we can establish deep connections with family and friends. We can become part of a community too. ——— But there are other times when we need to engage in restorative practices – creating healthy and nourishing meals, carving out a space to exercise, meditate or contemplate, enjoying the benefits of a long bath and giving our bodies the sleep they need. Love, too. Our homes should always be open to love.

'One's destination is never a place but rather a new way of looking at things.'
Henry Miller

BELONGING

There are many beautiful places to live in the world, and we all hope to find a place to call our own. Sometimes it seems preordained – when we choose to settle where we were born and our family remains. Often we stay on this path because we enjoy the ongoing connections with those that are near and dear to us. And we have nurtured relationships in our local community.

Other times we seek out a new world, one that feels more aligned with our values. Cities that reward hard work or innovation. Countries that support families. Or even small towns that embrace a slower way of living. But wherever we choose to establish our roots, we enhance the experience when we engage in the life around us.

When we belong to a community we feel a level of acceptance of who we are and the choices we have made. A sense of worth also evolves when we develop intimate relationships, and give and receive love. We deepen connections within our community when we become active participants, from engaging with our neighbours, to supporting local businesses. We can literally build these relationships with our design choices, and how we nurture our surrounding environment. There are many ways to create a sense of belonging.

Community can begin at home too. When we sit down together as a family over a meal, we form emotional bonds. When we pass food around the table, and listen with intent, we create lifelong connections. When we set aside life's many distractions and focus on family, we signal our priorities.

'Environments are not passive wrappings, but are, rather, active processes which are invisible.'
Marshall McLuhan

Connect to the surrounding spaces

Where we dwell is one part of where we live. Every day often involves some sort of journey through our surrounding environment. We become intimate with the nuances of our areas – the gradual developments along streetscapes and the slow change of the seasons. When we take the time to connect with our surrounding spaces, our lives become richer. We appreciate the impermanence of beauty, the passing of time, and how even the smallest changes can make a big difference.

Harmony

There are all sorts of benefits when we live in harmony with our environment. We all know about the long-term global advantages, but it also produces daily benefits for our general wellbeing. Spending time outdoors is good for our bodies – it gets them moving, reduces stress, and creates a sense of belonging. We can feel more connected to our landscape, regardless of whether it's urban, rural or coastal, when we nurture it – such as encouraging flora and fauna that help the local ecosystem.

The great outdoors is also somewhere we can daydream, and step out of our daily habits and thought patterns. There are no barriers or reminders of the material world. When it's just us and nature we can tune in to ourselves and our inner thoughts. It's a natural tonic to daily living.

The Japanese have taken this idea one step further. The practice of 'forest bathing' or *shinrin-yoku* is becoming more widely adopted as way to improve health and a sense of wellbeing. It involves taking a walk in woodland to breathe in the fresh air, and benefit from phytoncides, which help lower blood pressure and glucose levels as well as relieve stress. Nature has many benefits, indoors and out.

Wholistic living

Living sustainably can not only enhance our way of living, but help us feel connected to the world at large. When we buy better quality goods, we are more likely to care for them, repair when necessary and pass down rather than throw out. When we preference natural and sustainable materials, we are helping to limit our ecological footprint. We extend a helping hand to workers around the world when we buy ethically and engage in fair trade. Living with less not only makes ecological and economic sense but is a great time saver too. The less we own, the less there is to tidy.

Expanse

When we connect to our surrounds, we expand our sense of space. Letting in light, a view, a skyscape, a breeze, the scent of the garden, and even the hustle and bustle of a city below can help us feel part of a larger community. The same can be said of our buildings when we create something that's sympathetic to our local environment. We identify with our community when we choose a visual language that's in keeping with our neighbours. We can imprint our values and a sense of identity on the structure, but considerate choices can help us to feel that we belong.

Dee Purdy &
Andrew Hoskin

LONDON, UK

'Home is about each one of us in the family enjoying and existing in every space. Nowhere is off limits to the girls. For me, it's not about accumulating objects but rather about stripping things back to those things that give us joy. That doesn't mean living with the bare minimum but rather living with things that give me pleasure to use, look at, be around. I relish homely rituals and I think that beautiful objects can enhance these.'

LONDON IS A LONG WAY from what was once home for Dee Purdy and Andrew Hoskin. They grew up in far-flung outposts of the British Empire – South Africa and Australia, respectively. But it was on a boat on the River Thames that they met, and together they have forged a new life in an old country. Since the arrival of daughters Limi, seven, and Claya, four, the couple have created a tight-knit family and a home that is a distillation of what they value – history, travel and storytelling.

'We may not have as much space in London as both Andrew and I grew up with, but as a result we live closely together as a family, and all get a say in our home,' Dee says. While young, the girls have engaged conversations with their parents, and move around their home with respect and admiration for the collections that are on display.

Dee doesn't keep household goods for special occasions. 'We use hand-stitched napkins at dinnertime and often put candles on the table,' she says. 'Our everyday cutlery is silverware sourced from London's wonderful antique markets, and the girls happily use the turntable to put a record on.'

Space is at a premium in their narrow but tall terrace in West London. The house that the family moved into about three years ago is three storeys high and comprises five bedrooms. Two are used as offices – one as a home studio for Dee's children's clothing business, Une Belle Epoque, and the other for Andrew, who runs a software development company. The girls share a light-filled room on the first floor and the remaining bedroom is for guests, which includes a rotation of family and friends who travel via long-haul flights and stay for extended periods.

However, this house is larger than the last. The family lived in another terrace only two streets away but outgrew it after the arrival of Claya. They owned that place, but decided to rent this one from a friend so Andrew could work from home and Dee could set up her clothing business.

As it's a rental, they aren't able to make structural changes, but they have added layers to make it their own. And Dee has used paint in engaging ways – a harlequin wall in the girls' room and circus stripes on their door. It's a way of living that was fostered during her own childhood. 'Both my parents encouraged creative expression through music, art, clothes, food, in fact, everything we did,' she says. It's something Dee is keen to pass on to her children. 'I'm happy when I have the time to create something with the girls,' she says. 'Whether it's laying a beautiful table, baking or building a den.' All of it is important.

Dee Purdy & Andrew Hoskin

Dee Purdy & Andrew Hoskin

What attracted you to this home?
Definitely the open-plan living space and how light it is even in the depths of dark, northern winters. But also because it's close to our community in Brackenbury Village, which means that we get to live a village existence in a big city. We walk to most places, have a fabulous butcher, baker and coffee shop on our doorstep, and we often bump into friends when we are out and about.

How does your home make you feel?
I feel relaxed when I walk through the door. We keep the space downstairs fairly clear of toys with vintage suitcases and toy boxes but it still feels like home for all four of us. And we have no issue with the girls leaping around on the couches.

What objects hold a special meaning for you?
I love to haul things back from travels so definitely everything that reminds me of a particular time and place in the world but also all our vintage objects found at markets or auction houses. Our dining room table is particularly special to me as I bought it for a pittance on an online auction site and the pictures were terrible. So I had no idea whether we were picking up a gem or something cheap and nasty. It turned out that it was this beautiful piece of solid, scrubbed pine and had been treasured by an elderly gentleman. He was so happy to hear that it was going to be our family table.

How do you choose which items enter your home?
I choose items based on their story, their patina and their material. I love stripped-back metals, mirrors, linen and vintage wood. For me, the piece has to have soul; a piece that I will always find a place for in my home rather than a passing fancy.

How often do you edit your home and its collections?
I am constantly editing. At the moment, it's about stripping things back to only the pieces that I love. Living with less but enjoying every object.

How has your style evolved over the years? What has stayed consistent?
I have consistently loved natural materials with an industrial style. Over time I have become more confident in my choices and in trying to choose items with a story – whether it's because they are vintage or made by a particular artisan.

What gets priority in your home?
Linen, good ingredients and filling it with good people. We are all happiest when the house is buzzing.

What drives your creative expression?
A big part of what inspires us is travelling. We both bring back ideas to feed into our homes, onto the dining room table and into our wardrobes.

What's your favourite space?
In summer, it's sitting in the garden in the evening, lit up by strings of lights and with the strong scent of white jasmine filling the air.

What do you think makes a welcoming home?
For me, it's a relaxed atmosphere where you feel just as comfortable sitting on the floor talking to your hosts as kicking off your shoes and curling your legs up onto a chair.

Kim Baarda

AMSTERDAM, NETHERLANDS

'Home is where my family is. I need my favourite furniture and art pieces – and it's important
they have the right space in our home – but above all home will always be a place where
I can rest, laugh and spend precious time with my boys, family and dear friends.'

AFTER TWENTY-TWO YEARS OF LIVING OVERSEAS, Kim Baarda felt the call of home. While she had created beautiful spaces in Israel and London over the years, Kim wanted to return to the country of her birth, the Netherlands. 'I wanted my sons to experience a slower pace of life, and more of the childhood that Amsterdam could offer us compared with the rushed and pressurised lifestyle of London,' she says.

At the end of summer in 2016 she moved into her apartment with sons David, twelve, and Jeffrey, nine. Kim was drawn to the location as it was still quite central but far enough away from the tourists who flock to the historical centre. Also, the place had been renovated and was ready for her to move in. 'As we were moving from another country that was a big tick,' she says. 'It was easy to make it into a cosy home so we could concentrate first of all on settling into a new life in Amsterdam.' Kim was also drawn to the high ceilings, open-plan downstairs living and the small garden, which can be hard to find in the city.

A veteran of moving house, Kim has learnt what should take priority when setting up a new home. 'I always believe I can make any space into a homely home with the pieces I have collected over the years,' she says. 'It is an organic process for me as some things will over the years be replaced with new favourite pieces, but there are some core items I will always adore and find a place for no matter where we live or move to next.'

Kim says that hanging favourite pieces of art, and furnishing a home with rugs, can help to create a sense of home quickly. She finds the process quite instinctive. 'I am very emotional,' Kim says. 'So when I love a piece, I am convinced I will find a place for it.' However, she is sensitive to when the interior decor is not working cohesively. 'I get very obsessed if something does not look right, which can be even a small vase or some pieces of furniture together,' Kim says. 'I will spend my weekend or evenings rearranging until I feel it works and flows. I am quite obsessive in that sense. It can bother me for weeks or days when some small item feels out of place or clashes with other colours or art pieces – I have to get it right.'

Ultimately, though, her priority is being with her boys and enjoying meals together. 'The spaces and objects will be done in my spare time,' Kim says. 'We are big foodies.' She often cooks and bakes with her eldest son, and the family eats at the dining table or outside when the weather is good. Even better if family or friends join them. That is her idea of a happy home.

Q / A

What attracted you to this home?
It is a fantastic location: still in the centre of Amsterdam but a bit away from all the eight million tourists, who descend on Amsterdam annually.

What changes did you make?
Not many, as we only arrived a year ago and have concentrated on settling in to life, school and work in Amsterdam. My children were born and raised in London, so the Netherlands is new to them. I would love to change the location of the kitchen, which is now at the front of the apartment, but I would move it around to the back and have the living room at the front. And I will definitely change the bathroom. It is now very dark and typically Dutch with mosaic black tiles.

How does your home make you feel?
A place to gather with my family and friends. Sharing good and bad times and most of all lots of laughter. It is my family which makes the home feel like a home.

What objects hold a special meaning for you?
I love my art pieces. Most of them have been carefully collected over the last twenty years or so and some have been made for or given to me by dear friends. I also have a whole collection of drawings, which are made by David and Jeffrey's grandfather from Paris, to commemorate special events in the boys' lives like birthdays or holidays, even the start of their new school in Amsterdam. We love them and they hold a special place in our hearts. There is always excitement when a new drawing by Grandpa Gilbert and Grandma Suzie arrives in the post. We have started mixing in with them black and white pictures of loved ones, some still amongst us, some passed away but still very much cherished in our hearts.

How often do you edit your home and its collections?
I think a house and its interiors should evolve and change over time. So I regularly replace or rearrange our living room and the bedrooms. Of course, there are some key pieces, such as an antique Dutch 400-year-old linen cupboard, which was given to me by a dear friend, that I would love to keep for a long time to come.

How has your style evolved over the years?
Even when I was younger I loved interior design, but I just could not afford good-quality pieces. I discovered over time that I love using and restoring old furniture and mixing it in with more modern pieces. About ten years ago I started collecting mid-century modern furniture pieces. Some I have sold again, but some key pieces, like my high sideboard, salon table and drinks cabinet, I will keep for a long time to come. I also love splashes of colour and play with different geometric patterns – not just with the cushions I have on my sofa and chairs, but also in rugs or by reupholstering one chair in a red colour. I have been tossing with the idea of going more plain but I always get drawn back to colour and especially geometric patterns.

Which materials are important to you?
I love wool and linens, and upholstery fabrics.

What gets priority in your home?
Oh, definitely meals! I also love looking at all our collections on the wall as some remind me of people I love or fond memories of holidays.

What's your favourite space?
Our living room, gathering around the living room table with a good glass of wine, fire on and playing board games with the boys.

When are you happy at home?
When we are all together and eating good food, with some friends or family to join us.

What do you think makes a welcoming home?
People, but also personally picked pieces that hold dear memories or have been carefully collected over the years. I do not believe you can decorate a home in a short space of time and buy all your furniture and art at once. I love to collect pieces of art and furniture over time and do not keep to one style. I mix and match periods and styles.

How do you personalise your home?
I love making and creating things. I embroider my own cushions, make headboards for my sons' bedrooms, restore old furniture and bring pieces back to life. For me that gives a personal touch to what would otherwise be just any other home.

BALANCE

Many of the questions we ask in relation to our homes relate to achieving some form of balance in our lives. How should we spend our time and money? What do we prioritise now and defer until later? Do we renovate next year or when the children are older, the business is doing better, or our salaries are higher? How much do we spend on furniture, fittings and decorative objects? Should we indulge today and gain a lifetime's worth of enjoyment or save and wait until we have paid off a mortgage or other expenses? And how do we make time for our home life, and its ongoing maintenance, in amongst competing interests that relate to work, children, family, health and leisure?

Perhaps we don't have to choose between competing interests. Instead we can look to the rhythms of nature – there's a season for thrift and a season for abundance, a time for growth and a time for rest. When we focus on our needs, and what's important in this day, month or season of our lives, we can create our own rhythms to make decisions more easily.

Of course, achieving a balanced life takes work – the discipline of keeping to habits that support our priorities and values. We should ask can our homes support sustainable lifestyle choices? Are they easy to maintain, is there somewhere quiet to meditate, is there a place to connect with our family?

Balance at home contributes to our sense of wellbeing. When rooms breathe we feel at ease. When objects are placed in harmony, they can create a calming effect. Materials, textures, light and sound all add to the atmosphere too. We create our best homes when we design for the heart and not just the shell.

'The secret is balance: instead of doing everything faster, do everything at the right speed. Sometimes fast. Sometimes slow. Sometimes in between.'

Carl Honoré

Stay focused

We create a home to enhance our lives every day. However, over time our needs and tastes change. We add to our collections, accumulate more objects and use spaces in different ways. Sometimes we can also become disenchanted with our home life or fall into a rut. Our space can reflect last year's needs, not today's. But when we create an adaptable space, it can accommodate the changes in our lives. And when we focus on what makes us happy at home, we can give our life meaning.

Decision-making

When we have a clear vision of what we want for our lives, decision-making becomes easy. It doesn't matter what stage we're at, when we prioritise what matters most, we can find our answers. At home we might prefer to wait for the right pieces rather than buy something that does not fit with our values. Or make a compromise that still feels as if it maintains integrity – perhaps buying a quality second-hand piece rather than a cheap new product that may end up in landfill. Decision-making is a skill, and the more we practise staying our course, the better we become at it.

Less

We can feel liberated when we live with less. It's a lesson that comes into focus when we go on holiday or pack up our home for a move or before a renovation. How little we actually need! When we return to our home we can view our possessions with fresh eyes. We can take this opportunity to rid our homes of all that is superfluous and the pieces that never really were part of our story. Living simply comes with benefits too. When we create a home that's easy to maintain, everyone can participate and the job gets done more quickly.

Principles

Making a home is as much about household management as interior design. It can be complex, especially when multiple people are involved. However, when we sit down together and agree on what's important to making our home life work, we can use that goal as a guide for day-to-day living. If we want to create a happy, kind and respectful home, we can define these qualities and ask for everyone's agreement to live by these principles. When we create a home where everyone can feel loved, valued, safe and secure, we will meet our collective needs.

One word

Sometimes what we leave out of a space speaks as much about our values as what is inside. However, one of the hardest words to say in the modern-day world is 'no'. No to our phones and screens and technology. No to buying more clothes and accessories and homewares and gadgets. But when we say no we become more aware of what's really important. When we say no our resolve becomes stronger. When we say no more often, we can gain back some of our most precious commodities: time and money.

Pierre Emmanuel Martin & Stéphane Garotin

LYON, FRANCE

'Home is the place where we feel comfortable, surrounded by our souvenirs of our travels around the world. Good music, a good glass of wine, good food – this is how we consider life.'

PIERRE EMMANUEL MARTIN & Stéphane Garotin have made a career out of creating beautiful interiors as the French design duo Maison Hand. But to them, a home is about creating a space where you can share memorable moments. 'Nothing makes us more happy than cooking and having a nice, simple lunch or dinner with our families and friends,' Pierre says.

Stéphane is a keen cook and the couple take pleasure in meal preparations. 'Shopping at the market for food, it is always a great moment,' Pierre says. 'We can spend hours preparing food for others.' They also enjoy setting the table with various pieces that they have bought from all over the world. Thought is given to the mix of plates, glasses and accessories they use, and flowers or plants are always present. 'We always buy them, even when we are alone,' Pierre says. 'It is part of our way of life.'

The home they have created in the French city of Lyon is an example of their work at large. But it is not something that can be replicated. 'Our customers like to come to our home to see our work and so often they ask us to re-create the look at their place,' Pierre says. 'But we can't. Because this place is us and our DNA. We can help them select the pieces of furniture but we cannot select for them a book that we like – they have to choose the pieces that mean something to them. For example, someone might ask us how should we place some lights together, and we say, "It has to feel right for you."'

The couple moved into the apartment in 2015, drawn to the size and scale of the rooms, as well as the traditional detailing on almost every surface – from the panelled walls to the parquetry floorboards and shuttered windows. The south-facing aspect was also appealing, as was a courtyard at the centre of the apartment that all the windows overlooked. But rooms were repositioned to suit their lifestyle, such as turning the dining room into a kitchen so that it could be more central to the home.

'But this has taken twenty years to collect,' Pierre says, pointing to an extensive collection of art, books, decorative objects, and furniture. And all of it has meaning for them. Pierre can recall the first piece of art he saved to buy, and the same with every item of furniture. That is what makes it a home, he says. 'Your home has to be for you.' And he is sanguine about the fact that everyone has to start somewhere, believing that the enjoyment comes with creating your own story.

Pierre Emmanuel Martin & Stéphane Garotin

Q / A

When did you move here and why?
We moved into this apartment in October 2015 because we were looking for a bigger home full of light.

What attracted you to this home?
We were so seduced by the light, the size of the windows, the balcony and the central courtyard which makes you your own neighbour. It is south exposed and has a balcony. We also fell in love with its Haussmannian style, which is so French.

What changes did you make?
We changed almost everything. The kitchen became a guest bedroom, the dining room became a kitchen and we created two extra bathrooms.

What didn't you want to change?
The flooring, the fireplaces and the doors.

What objects hold a special meaning for you?
Our collection of baskets in the kitchen on the shelves.

How do you choose which items enter your home?
Feeling. Most of the time we bring back some objects or artwork from our journeys. In Japan recently, we bought many ceramics. For furniture, we try to have comfortable couches and armchairs. When we do not find what we are looking for we design our own pieces, such as the sofas in our living room. We like to mix old pieces with contemporary ones and iconic items as well.

How often do you edit your home and its collections? What's involved in the process?
We try to change every two years to a completely different atmosphere. We can go from a very bright place to a very dark one such as our previous home. This time we feel so good in our apartment that we have decided to stay here, but we are already working on different colour codes and new furniture and curtains.

How has your style evolved over the years? What has stayed consistent?
Well, actually when we look back on our projects, it is obvious that we still have the same DNA. We have always privileged natural materials and light colours. We have never been into projects that are very colourful. Even if we like colours when we go to a hotel or restaurant or friend's home, we feel more peaceful in light environments. Nevertheless, we are always open to new designs, shapes and materials. We have always liked accumulations and it is something you can find in all our projects.

Which materials are important to you?
Wood, stone, linen, wool, ceramic.

What's your favourite space?
The kitchen. It is where you share the most beautiful moments with your lover and your friends.

What makes you happy at home?
Light and flowers.

Cassandra Karinsky

MARRAKECH, MOROCCO

'Home is a place to be calm, a sanctuary. I'm in the souk so much and it
can be exhausting. I'm transported out of the chaos of Marrakech. It's an escape,
and a soothing and calming environment. When I first moved here there were days
when I was burnt out but now I'm more content because I've got a more solid home.
I've put more of an effort into making it comfortable for myself. And I can
have friends come and hang out. That's important for me.'

MOROCCO IS ONE OF THOSE COUNTRIES that can have a strong hold on people. The first time Cassandra Karinsky visited was in 1996 when she was on holiday with a friend. At the time, she was keen to open her own restaurant and stayed in Morocco for about five months exploring options. However, she returned to Sydney and ended up working at leading restaurants Tetsuya and Bills. 'But I knew I had to come back,' she says. 'There was always something about Morocco that made me want to return.'

After many research trips she packed her bags for good in 2005. She started making kaftans, then opened a shop in Marrakech. The restaurant idea got put on hold after she also started a personal shopping business with another friend. At the same time Cassandra was styling photo shoots with a French photographer and often borrowing rugs from the souks. Soon she started her own business, Kulchi, focusing on sourcing rugs for interior designers and clients around the world.

While Cassandra runs the showroom in a souk in the medina, she lives beyond the old city walls. 'When people first move here they get caught up in the romanticism of the medina, but for me it's so insular,' she says. 'They might do it for a couple of years but all of my friends have moved out into properties on the outside. It's a classic scenario – they do a medina and riad and then they are over it.'

She lives close to the conveniences of a big city but also the smells, sounds and sights that are synonymous with Marrakech. 'You have guys on the street coming around with their wheelbarrows selling blueberries, raspberries and strawberries, and big wheelbarrows of figs,' she says. 'It's more like a modern city but you still have the provedores with produce from their farm.'

Cassandra moved into her current home about three years ago. It's her second apartment out of the medina. 'I could see the potential. And loved the light,' she says. 'A lot of the old properties are being pulled down. It's hard to find really character-filled places.'

To freshen the rental, Cassandra had the walls and floors painted. 'Everyone thinks I just do white,' she says. 'But the souk is so intense that I needed something soothing and calm.' She also added doors to the balcony where there had been a window, and retiled the kitchen. The furniture was mostly custom made using contacts she knew through her businesses. 'You have to design and make every-thing here,' Cassandra says. It's a process that takes time and involves trial and error but she has created a place where she can live, work and entertain.

'There are moments when I'm walking to the souk for work and I think, I am so fortunate,' she says. 'I love my lifestyle. I love what my company has given me – the ease to move around and travel. There are so many opportunities here. It can be difficult at times but there is freedom too and that is liberating.'

Cassandra Karinsky

Cassandra Karinsky

Q / A

What gets priority in your home?
Entertaining is big. I wanted the dining area to be the focal point. The table – it's where most of us gravitate to. I can fit fifteen people around here. And I enjoy cooking.

What objects hold a special meaning for you?
I'm not that possessive about material things. I can let things go quite easily. I think it's always nice to start fresh. I gave everything away from my last apartment. I have always been very minimal. I don't have much clutter.

How has your style evolved over the years?
I think it's the same. Since being here I have enjoyed visiting flea markets and finding vintage pieces and incorporating them into my space. I enjoy pairing them with more modern clean items. My first apartment here felt more transient. It was a more minimal Moroccan style with mattresses on the floor. This place feels more permanent and I have put more effort into making it a home.

What's your favourite space?
Sometimes I put my work on the table and enjoy looking out to the palm tree and the jacaranda – it reminds me a bit of Sydney. It's so beautiful here at dusk and I enjoy sitting out on the balcony with my neighbour.

What is life like here?
The lifestyle here is so easy. It doesn't feel that you have the pressures, such as in Australia, about how you think society perceives you. It is a very laidback lifestyle. You go to dinner here and people are talking about their projects – there are more creative juices flowing. It's also so accessible to Europe. I visit Paris and Madrid a lot, and go to Portugal quite a bit too. Here you can set your own rhythm and do what you want.

'Living here you feel grateful for what you've got. It puts things into perspective. Every night I write down three things I'm grateful for. If you don't you just lose ... you don't see the good things. You get caught up with keeping up with the Joneses. Half of the stuff that people buy, it's not for their own soul but to show other people. That's the one thing I'll always take from Morocco – how humbling it's been.'

Cassandra

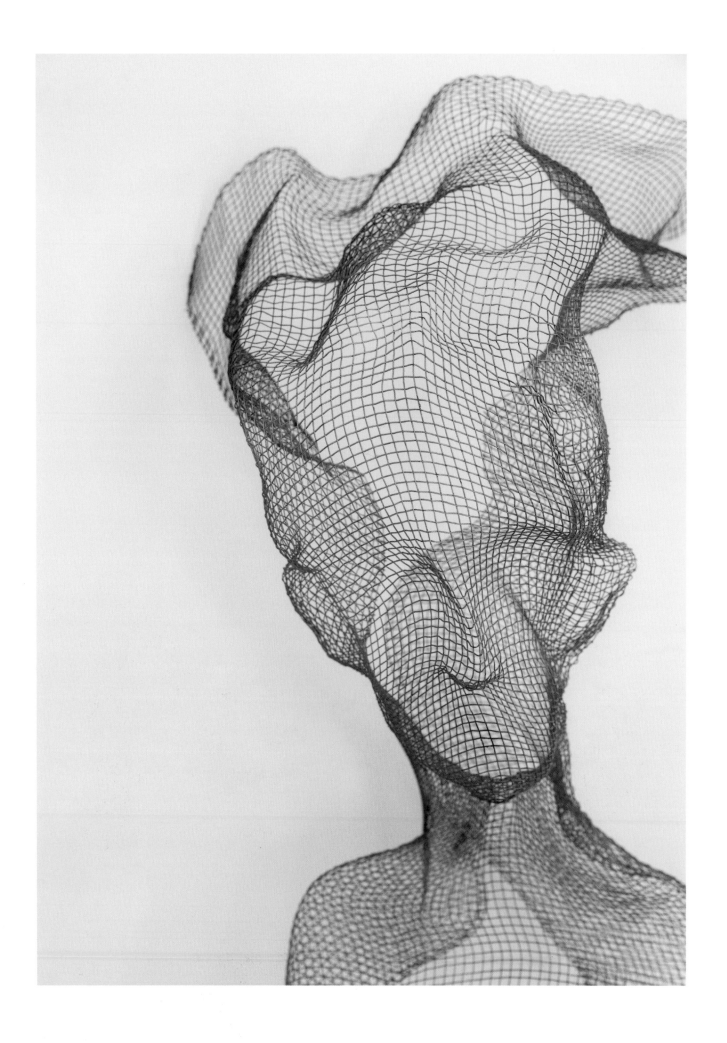

INGENUITY

Ideas are unique and distinctive when we create from the heart, our place of truth. Our home becomes authentic and engaging when it tells something of our lives, and expresses our soul in what we see, touch and feel. However, when we design spaces to look original, they often become derivative. It is when we focus on our needs that the result is like no other.

'Soul' derives from the Greek word *psychē* meaning 'to breathe' and relates to the essence of a person – our character, feelings, memories and reasoning. When we engage with these elements, we start to express the purest form of ourselves. Focusing on what nourishes our soul also helps to bring our home to life.

When we pursue our passion for art, textiles, travel, fashion or books, we awaken our space. Rich decorative layers start to form because we want to experience what brings pleasure daily. When we want to see, touch and feel our collections, we create a place of interest – not for others, but ourselves. When we want to enjoy them regardless of our circumstances or resources, we tap into that inner well of originality known as ingenuity.

Ingenuity is creativity born out of necessity. It is an opportunity to play and can manifest in many ways around our homes, from the structures we build to the materials we use. We create poetic solutions when we try to solve problems based on meeting our needs. And the more we delve into our interests, the more we are exposed to new ways of being. We start to move away from the collective consciousness and form our own ideas. When we adapt them to our spaces, we live authentically.

'To know what you prefer, instead of humbly saying Amen to what the world tells you you ought to prefer, is to have kept your soul alive.'

Robert Louis Stevenson

Be adaptable

Homes are living spaces, always in a state of change. Yet adaptability is often overlooked even though families grow, children's needs change, our needs change. Relationships develop or dissipate and job roles expand and contract. When our homes evolve alongside us, we create a space rich in beauty that has formed through the layers of life.

Break the rules

If we want to design our homes according to a rule book, there are plenty around. But to make a home we need to focus on our needs, and create with our own circumstances and environment in mind. If a living room is redundant, we can repurpose it. If family meals are a large affair, we can supersize our table. If a kitchen is where we live, we can make it feel more like a living space. And as our needs change, so can our rooms.

Fluidity

Perfection can be pernicious when it comes to interiors. It has a way of weaving its way into our ideas of what a home should be. But beauty is often created in imperfect moments – unexpected arrangements, when the ordinary is elevated to the extraordinary, and fortuitous discoveries. When we open our minds to new possibilities, we can create spaces that are poetic, kinetic, dynamic – sometimes all in the same space.

Rethink

It is natural to want the best for our home. But when we are designing spaces, that can become expensive. Where do we draw the line? Which products and materials do we prioritise? Maybe we should rethink the way we create, and our ideas on what will make us happy. There is a lot to be said for humble materials. When we use them proudly or in a new or unexpected way, they can create a beautiful statement. They can create interest through their application. Or become a simple backdrop to other material layers.

Repurpose

Objects and materials are the starting point for any interior design. But we don't always have to use something for its original purpose. When we let our needs lead the way, we can discover many ingenious solutions and even the most basic handy skills can result in custom pieces. Likewise, when we find something we love, we can repurpose it. A vintage door can become the top of a coffee or dining table. Tiles can be used on a kitchen benchtop. Even subtler differences can work – floor tiles on walls. Outdoor taps inside. When we create with our needs in mind – for purpose and pleasure – the solution will look and feel authentic.

Editing

Our homes benefit from editing regularly. The flotsam of our days can quickly take centre stage. But we want to see the pieces that produce the most pleasure. While corralling the bric-a-brac of daily living into beautiful bowls and baskets can help, we can take other steps to create harmony at home. When we prioritise beauty for even the simplest and most functional objects, we can create a calmer and more pleasing environment. When packaging is attractive, it matters less if it is left on display. We can find joy when we create poetry in the everyday.

Arabella &
Sam McIntosh

LOS ANGELES, USA

'Home is an extension of our family and our personalities. It's a place for playing music too loud, reading, laughter, tantrums, skateboarding, cooking and eating together, nights by the fire with friends drinking wine. It's where I feel safe, relaxed and happy.'

ARABELLA AND SAM MCINTOSH moved from Bondi Beach on the east coast of Australia to California on the west coast of the USA about two years ago – with just a suitcase each and their son Bobby's favourite toys and books. Since relocating they have also welcomed daughter Willa into their family. To see them through the early months a friend lent them some furniture. 'We made a conscious decision to only buy pieces for the house that we would be excited to unpack out of a container later down the track,' Arabella says. 'Keeping in mind that we won't be here forever, we bought with purpose, and we bought forever.'

Everything in their home tells a little piece of their story since moving across the Pacific Ocean for Sam's work as the owner and publisher of surf magazine *Stab*. 'It's important that I have a connection to everything in my home,' says Arabella, the designer behind sustainable homewares brand Palm Beach Black. 'Each piece will always remind me of the new places I discovered and people I met sourcing them. Such as the trips with friends to flea markets in Long Beach, squeezing an outdoor fireplace from Costa Mesa into the car, and the crazy cat lady named Dolly who sold me the antique captain chairs that I have in the dining room.

I have learnt so much about the culture and the people and the areas of this city through getting the pieces.'

Provenance is something that's dear to Arabella. She grew up living above her family's antique store in Sydney's Balmain. Many items in their home were in constant rotation with the shop. 'It looked incredible but, of course, I longed for simplicity and modern furniture – pieces that people hadn't owned,' she says. 'The older I get I can't help but gravitate towards vintage or handmade objects that have had previous chapters.'

Sam has a strong sense of his own style and outlook too. 'Sam likes to live lean,' Arabella says. 'He believes that a life overloaded with belongings can stop you from living. This philosophy helps me curate my collections so when we put everything together it doesn't feel too overwhelming.'

The couple's home is now almost at capacity. In their previous place they had a 'one-in, one-out' policy for purchases. For now, Arabella enjoys the process of working with what they've got. 'I am a massive midnight furniture shuffler,' she says. 'It's what my mum and I did when I was growing up. Even when I visit my mum we do all of our creative stuff at night. A house is a living extension of yourself – it's always evolving.'

'The rules are that any new piece we buy is not going to end up on the side of the road – that we will still love it in ten years' time.'

Arabella

Arabella & Sam McIntosh

Arabella has not only made furniture
for her home, but decorative items too,
such as the mobile that hangs above her
daughter's cot.

Q / A

What attracted you to this home?
The curved rock wall and square picture window next to it. Moving to California, it felt authentic and unlike anything we could have found in Sydney. Part of the brief was to have an experience that we wouldn't have at home.

What didn't you want to change?
The kitchen. It's original and quirky. It's definitely not something I would install myself but it's warm and has the feeling that it's been a central organ in the home for a long time.

How does this home make you feel?
Centred. At ease. Because of the neutral tones in here – it really affects my mood because I'm such a visual person.

What objects hold a special meaning for you?
The table. The dining area was important to us because we always eat together as a family. We also do a lot of entertaining. I had it custom-made – it's 1 metre (3.2 feet) wide – a lot of people said it would be too big but I wanted this size because I like to put plates in the middle when we are entertaining.

How do you choose which items enter your home?
The rules are that any new piece we buy is not going to end up on the side of the road – that we will still love it in ten years time. And nothing disposable. If I ring Sam about something I'm considering buying, he asks, 'Will we still love it when we take it out of the shipping container?' More recently I've been asking myself, is this something that will be worthy of handing down to our kids? We also try to buy things that we wouldn't be able to get in Australia.

How often do you edit your home and its collections?
Every day I rearrange things. Our friend Tom says that every time he comes over something has changed.

How has this area influenced your ideas on the home?
California has been in drought for so long that they are experts in sustainable low-water garden designs. I have always been interested in garden design but now I am obsessed with desert gardens.

Which materials are important to you?
Wood, linen, jute, wool, mud cloth and there's always lots of denim in our house – I love the way it fades and improves with age.

What's your favourite space?
Around the fireplace. We have had so many beautiful evenings there as a family, listening to music or reading. In winter we enjoy having friends over and sitting around the fire. What's also nice about this house is that it is really inclusive and warm. In our previous apartment we didn't have many places to sit and entertain. The house was really well designed with the bedrooms quite separate from the living area. We have lots of guests come to stay so it was important that we chose a house where people don't feel like they're on top of each other and feel relaxed while they are here.

When are you happy at home?
When I'm hanging out in the backyard with the kids. I don't feel like I have to rush out of the house all the time.

What makes a welcoming home?
I think texture in building materials, furniture and textiles. Music. Having casual seating options makes people feel relaxed. I like having layered rugs and floor cushions that encourage people to sit on the floor and lounge around. Having a space that's clean and tidy – but one that looks lived in. I think when things are too clean and clinical they can feel cold and uncomfortable and people can't relax in the space. No one wants to sit on a cold hard chair in a perfect silent house. Also, having natural or soft lighting is important. Here the light is so good – every afternoon is the same – it's the Hollywood light. In the evening using lamps or pendants with linen or rattan shades, which provide soft diffused lighting, makes the space feel warm and inviting.

Virgine Batterson

SYDNEY, AUSTRALIA

'We love the home we have created for our family. My home is where my family is –
a collection of moments. We all get involved with the changes we make in our home,
everyone's opinion matters.'

BEAUTY IS MORE THAN SKIN DEEP in the home of Virgine and Scott Batterson. The couple, who live in Avalon on Sydney's Northern Beaches with their three children, Kenyon, eighteen, Ella, fourteen, and Liam, ten, are creating a home like no other. While they say it's in a state of renovation and unfolding slowly, as much as their busy lives allow while Virgine runs her nearby clothing store Mamapapa, its execution is seemingly without parallel.

Everything that Virgine touches is beautiful – even a make-do kitchen that will one day be ripped out. 'Yes, I love looking at beautiful things,' she says. 'Who wouldn't?' But not everyone prioritises enhancing their surrounds today. While others may endure a clumsy space or insensitive material choices, it's important to Virgine that spaces meet her inner needs. 'It's the creative inside of me,' she says. 'I feel happy, productive and alive – these are my elements.'

When the family bought a 1970s chalet-style house at the end of 2013, Virgine wanted to make some changes straight away before they even started to contemplate renovations. She wanted a blank slate so that they could make the space their own. Within three days the whole family helped to rip out the entire kitchen, carpet and bathroom and to paint almost non-stop so they could move in before Christmas.

'I remember I was so busy in the store and Kenyon surprised me, and found a huge branch and walked home with it, and put it up for me before I got home,' she says. 'It was unreal. I was so happy as we had no idea where our ornaments were in the move. So we all took flowers and leaves and sprayed them with snow. It was the best ever.'

Since that initial burst of activity, the couple have made many non-structural changes. In the kitchen, they inserted a ceramic sink into a trestle table and created a temporary timber shelving system. Large-scale family photos have gone on display. Keepsakes sourced from flea markets in France and the US have been placed on show as reminders of Virgine's life growing up in France, and of her time spent living in the US, where she met Scott.

But even more important than beauty is family. The space that Virgine is creating is for her children, and their memories. 'My kids will always be my priority,' she says. And while being surrounded by *objets d'art* brings Virgine happiness, of greater importance is creating a home that her children will remember. 'I want them to appreciate details, to see outside and behind the box. I want them to look at things differently, and to understand the story behind it.'

Virgine Batterson

When did you move into this house and why did you move here?
We moved end of December 2013, just a few days before Christmas. It was hectic but all worth it. We fell in love and saw the potential – house with a view and just a stroll from the beach. It was a dream come true.

Why did you choose this particular place?
It ticked a lot of boxes – lots of spaces with charm, many small hiding rooms and a garden, but it needed a complete makeover. Also, it was very close to Mamapapa store. The kids instantly loved it, and so did we.

What changes did you make and why?
We are always making changes, and will be for a while. The first thing we did was to rip up the carpet. We found floorboards underneath, and painted the entire interior white, to make it lighter. The house was really dark to start with. The house has such an eclectic feel about it but we want to make it our own.

How does your home make you feel?
Our home has endless opportunities – it brings out my creativity.

What objects hold a special meaning for you?
I have so many objects I love, to be honest, but my photos will be the most important family treasures. As for objects, I have to say my wire vintage lockers.

How do you decide which objects enter your home?
If my husband could answer this he would say, it has to be heavy, rusty, old, vintage or white. For me an object has to speak to me, or have a meaning, a story or simply make me smile.

How often do you edit your home, your collections and what's on display?
All the time, weekly, things move around. Objects can have a different meaning, style or story in different places of the house, and I love that.

How has your style evolved over the years? What has stayed consistent? What has changed?
I believe my style has evolved as I'm getting older. I love the idea of being more of a minimalist, or I think I do. I have always loved industrial features and raw furniture. And white has always been my favourite colour of all time – that has been consistent.

Which materials are important to you?
I love raw materials – concrete, wood, linen – anything with raw texture.

What are your essentials in your home?
My children always come first. But when it comes to my home, I love my linens – bed linen and my white floaty curtains. I couldn't imagine living without them.

What's your favourite space?
Depends on the season, in winter we are always all around the fireplace, playing games, loving the warm cosy ambience. In summer, we love the pool area, it's beautiful and super fun.

When are you happy at home?
I love our home. We have lots to do but we are happy when each project comes alive.

KINDNESS

Sometimes the hardest person to be kind to is ourselves. We are so busy trying to create meaningful lives, happy children, beautiful homes, all while living sustainably. We fill our days with lists and goals. We multi-task and are never far from technology or connectivity. It is little wonder that wellbeing continues to grow as a health movement.

We are in a bind though. Our brains are wired to hunt and improve upon the status quo yet we live in a world of over-abundance – not only of produce and products, but our exposure to them. Stress levels are rising yet we are working less. Average working hours have fallen in every country for which the OECD has data. But the glorification of 'busy' continues. We are a product of the information age, and it surrounds us relentlessly.

Somehow we need to get back to our natural order – channelling our needs and drives towards activities that improve our lives. Growing our own produce, or at least eating foods free from preservatives and additives. Nurturing a home where we can give and receive love and respect. Creating social connections in the real world. When we find meaning in life, we can reach our full potential.

Our home can provide the framework to create happiness in our lives. Within its walls we can slow down to focus on our natural rhythms. We can create time for quiet contemplation. These are acts of kindness we can start today.

'People look for retreats for themselves, in the country, by the coast, or in the hills …
There is nowhere that a person can find a more peaceful and trouble-free retreat than in his own mind …
So constantly give yourself this retreat and renew yourself.'

Marcus Aurelius

Nurture yourself

We spend a lot of time and attention on making and changing spaces, but it is important to learn how to enjoy them. Our homes can function as a place to rest our bodies, rejoice in our relationships and restore our values.

Rest

Rest comes in many forms, although the most powerful is sleep. While research continues to advocate about eight hours a night for adults, many of us don't make sleep a priority despite the destructive knock-on effects – weakened immunity, weight gain, increased risk for diabetes and heart disease, and more. Extended periods without sleep may lead to irreversible brain damage too, as well as increase our risk of an early death. What's stopping us going to bed? Bedtime rituals are key, and should include turning off devices at least half an hour before sleep as they suppress sleep-inducing melatonin production. However, luxurious linen, a feather-filled quilt, and a good book are all incentives to go to bed.

Relax

Bathing has long been part of cultural life, and has as much to do with relaxing as cleaning. The Romans made it an art form while the idea of the Turkish bath house and its therapeutic benefits has spread throughout the world. The restorative effects of bathing are part of Korean and Japanese cultures too. While most of these methods incorporate a steam room, there's nothing quite like the warm welcome of a long, deep bath. It is said to improve our heart health, help us breathe more deeply and ease the aches and pains of muscles.

Revive

Daytime rest is possible through the practice of meditation. It is the superdrug that requires no medication, just twenty minutes of daily dedication. Not only does it decrease stress, anxiety and depression, but it also helps improve our health, self-control, productivity and memory, among many other benefits. And all it requires is somewhere quiet to sit. We can also engage in a more playful form of contemplation – daydreaming. When we allow our brains to wander they form new pathways, which can result in insights. This is why when we get a mental block, it's a good idea to go for a walk or change our activity. Something worth considering when we get stuck with decision-making in relation to our own homes.

Rejoice

Taking the time to connect with family or friends is important for our wellbeing. Our home provides the ideal setting, and the dining table is where we can nurture some of the most important and fulfilling relationships of our lives. Sharing family meals has positive effects on children too. They are more likely to do better at school, less likely to use drugs or alcohol later in life and less likely to become overweight, not to mention the nutritional benefits. The table is where lifelong memories are made.

Restore

Meeting our human and emotional needs is a journey that can begin at home. It is where we can find happiness and love, and create a life of meaning. Our home is also a nest and cocoon – a place to retreat and restore our bodies. It should feel inviting and comfortable and nurturing. Because if we can't feel that way in our home, where can we?

Vanessa Boz

'Our home is a reflection of us. We aren't trying to be anybody else through our home. It's an expression of our cultures and our travels. It's a legacy – there's a lot of sincerity in the way we create our home. I care a lot about the environment that we live in – and for my children to appreciate beauty. I want my children to see what I place a value on. And this home is where we come to reconnect.'

ABOUT FIVE YEARS AGO Vanessa Boz decided she wanted to create a home that could ground her itinerant family. At the time, she was pregnant with her youngest son, Lior, and put herself on a mission to find a place in Provence, France, where her husband, Cheki, and their three children, Marcelo, eleven, Amalya, eight, and Lior, five, could create memories with their extended far-reaching family. The journey was a coming home of sorts too.

While Vanessa has been based in London for the past ten years, she was born in France. Her mother, who lives in Paris, is half-Italian and half-French while her father is Algerian. To add to the mix, Vanessa met Cheki, a Turkish man, at university in Boston while studying economics. Their journey continued in New York, where they were based for a decade before crossing the Atlantic to live in London. However, the pull of France was strong. 'It was important to have a place that was an anchor in my native country,' Vanessa says. 'We wanted somewhere that we could get together with our families and for our children to build memories together because we don't live in each other's respective countries.' Cheki's family lives in Istanbul while Vanessa has one brother in London and another in Paris.

The calling of a central home base was strong as Vanessa and her children travel regularly around the world. This is in part related to living in Europe where many destinations are only a short plane ride away, but also because she chronicles their adventures on the family travel website, BozAround. Much of the home is decorated with finds from their adventures, and reflects her career as a travel writer and entrepreneur. 'I've accumulated a lot in my life – rugs, tiles, and so on – all bought hoping to use them one day,' Vanessa says. 'This was the house to bring them all together.'

Many of the pieces are older than her children. A hammock in the balcony off her bedroom was bought from indigenous tribes in the Orinoco Delta when she was about nineteen years old and working in Venezuela. 'At the time I thought, maybe one day I might have a nice place to hang it in the sun,' she says. A piano in the living room was the one that she learnt on as a child. 'My mum didn't have much money and she saved for it,' Vanessa says. 'I'm glad that it's now here.'

The family comes here as often as they can – all of the summer holidays and long weekends too. It's an opportunity for the children to spend time with their grandmother, who catches a fast train down from Paris. 'We always have friends or family visiting here – from Turkey, from London. It's a wonderful meeting point,' Vanessa says. 'Everyone is always happy to come to Provence.'

'It was a house to gather all of our travel influences under one roof and reflect our histories and personalities.'

Vanessa

Vanessa Boz

In her bathroom, Vanessa created a finish similar to *tadelakt*, a plaster surface often used in Moroccan interiors. The living room's cement floors and their timber joins are original to the house.

Q / A

Why Provence?
It has a wonderful mix of everything we like: food, culture and scenery. We love the nature of Provence – and the scents of rosemary, thyme and lavender. It's very rural and green here. It's very quiet. And the weather is nice all year long.

What attracted you to this particular home?
I visited quite a few. I love the fact we have neighbours that are all locals but at the same time our neighbours are the horses, ponies and sheep. It's at the bottom of the Alpilles and close to all the hiking and bike trails. We can also bike to town to get a croissant for breakfast or to get an ice cream.

What didn't you want to change?
The living room. I love the floor and the big bay windows. It's a large congregating room – everyone can find an occupation, from my daughter playing the piano, to the children playing cards, and my husband reading a book. It's the heart of the house.

How do you choose which items enter your home?
I like objects with a story. Whether the story is the object itself or the discovery – I am very intuitive when it comes to designing. I am drawn to colours and texture. The research process is fairly organic. I don't have a mission and must find one thing.

How often do you edit your home and its collections?
I like to rework things into a new space and give them a new life. Everything that we have together is an aggregation of a story.

How has your style evolved over the years?
It's really the same. I've always been inspired by my mother's style – together with my world travels. When my friends come here they always say, 'It's typical Vanessa.' The house reflects me very much.

Which materials are important to you?
I really wanted to reclaim as much as possible. That was my theme for doing this house. Growing the house but organically, in a conscious way. So there is a lot of wood and some of it we found in the garage. We transformed the bathrooms with craftsmanship. I spent a lot of time researching to find the right concrete tiles for the flooring – I like the grain, the texture, the imperfection. They are supposed to be lined imperfectly – I'm drawn to that, when it shows how it's made.

When are you happy at home?
When I hear my children laughing in the garden.

'I care about everything I have sourced – with lots of dedication and love – but I also want it to be enjoyed.'

Vanessa

ABOUT THE AUTHOR

Natalie Walton is a writer and stylist for leading interiors and lifestyle magazines, as well as the owner of Imprint House, a shop that celebrates beauty in the everyday. Her work has appeared on the pages of international titles for *Elle Decoration, Livingetc* and *Harper's Bazaar*. In Australia, Natalie is a regular contributor to *Australian House & Garden, Country Style, Home Beautiful, Inside Out, Jones* and *Marie Claire,* and she was deputy editor of *Real Living* for about five years. Through the editorial content agency she runs with photographer Chris Warnes – Warnes & Walton – her work has been published across the globe. In many ways, this book has evolved from her much-respected design and arts journal, *Daily Imprint*, which was launched over ten years ago. For more about her projects, visit nataliewalton.com.

ABOUT THE PHOTOGRAPHER

Chris Warnes is a leading Australian interiors and lifestyle photographer. His work has featured in a range of publications including *Elle Decoration UK, Vogue Living* and *Belle*. Chris is a regular contributor to *Australian House & Garden, Home Beautiful* and *Inside Out*. He also works for a range of architectural and advertising clients, and is one half of the editorial content agency Warnes & Walton. Chris's fine art photography is available through Otomys. His portfolio can be viewed at chriswarnes.com.au.

CREDITS

This book has been brought to life by the beautiful and inspiring homes that belong to the following people.

Ameé Allsop
ameeallsop.com
p 20–29

Arabella & Sam McIntosh
palmbeachblack.com
p 202–209

Bernie Kelsey
p 168

Caitlin & Samuel
Dowe-Sandes
pophamdesign.com
p 42–47

Caroline Carter
@thatgirlcaroline07
p 100–109

Cassandra Karinsky
kulchi.com
p 71, 186–195, 196

Claire Delmar
clairedelmar.com.au
p 72–81, 99, 146

Danielle McEwan
tigmitrading.com
p 30, 33, 149

Dee Purdy &
Andrew Hoskin
unebellepoque.com
p 150–159

Heidi Daburger
havelieofbyronbay.com.au
p 127, 222

Irene Mertens
sukha.nl
p 70, 128–141

Katrin Arens
katrinarens.it
p 6, 110–123, 144

Kim Baarda
p 160–167

Marjolein Delhaas
marjoleindelhaas.com
p 52–61

Nicole Vatselias
lumuinteriors.com
p 124, 200–201

Paul & Sophie
Yanacopoulos-Gross
homestories.com
p 19, 48, 82–93, 171, 236

Pierre Emmanuel Martin &
Stéphane Garotin
maison-hand.com
p 1, 94, 172–185

Sarah Foletta
folettaarchitects.com
p 14, 18

Simone McEwan &
Patrik Bergh
simonemcewan.co.uk
p 34–41

Vanessa Boz
bozaround.com
p 97, 226–227, 228–235

Virgine Batterson
mamapapa.com.au
p 2–3, 12, 51, 64, 66, 98,
210–221

Special thanks also to
Kate Midda and
Kirsten Bookallil.

REFERENCES & FURTHER READING

A selection of books have inspired and influenced this one.

At Home by Bill Bryson (Black Swan)
A fascinating and in-depth history of our homes.

Big Magic by Elizabeth Gilbert (Bloomsbury)
A challenge to embrace our inner well of creativity.

Home is Where the Heart Is? by Ilse Crawford
(Quadrille Publishing)
A book that champions designing from the heart, and has inspired much of my thinking on ideas about the home.

In Praise of Shadows by Junichiro Tanizaki (Vintage)
An insight into Japanese aesthetics.

It's Not How Good You Are,
It's How Good You Want To Be by Paul Arden (Phaidon)
A guide to making the most of your life.

The Architecture of Happiness
by Alain de Botton (Penguin Books)
A philosophical examination of buildings,
and how they make us feel.

The Medium is the Massage by
Marshall McLuhan and Quentin Fiore;
coordinated by Jerome Agel (Penguin Books)
How we see the world around us.

The Poetics of Space
by Gaston Bachelard (Penguin Classics)
The role our homes play in our inner lives.

Thrive by Arianna Huffington (WH Allen)
Redefining what it means to be successful.

Wabi-Sabi for Artists, Designers, Poets & Philsophers
by Leonard Koren (Imperfect Publishing)
How a Japanese aesthetic embraces the beauty
of imperfection.

Ways of Seeing by John Berger (Penguin Classics)
An examination of the language of images.

FURTHER READING
Blink by Malcolm Gladwell (Little, Brown and Company)
Essentialism by Greg McKeown (Ebury Publishing)
Grit by Angela Duckworth (Scribner)
The Brain That Changes Itself by Norman Doidge (Scribe)
The Power of Habit by Charles Duhigg (Random House)
The Science of Happiness by Stefan Klein (Scribe)
The Seven Habits of Highly Effective People
    by Stephen R. Covey (Simon and Schuster)
Walden by Henry David Thoreau (Tarcher Perigree)

THANK YOU

Writing a book is something of a solitary pursuit, but its creation is a wholehearted collaborative effort. It would not be possible without the homeowners featured within these pages who opened their doors – and shared their stories – for this book and, over the years, for Warnes & Walton. To all these people, I am eternally grateful. To Chris Warnes, for your incredible photos, and for joining me on this wild journey across countries and continents, I cannot thank you enough. To Evi Oetomo, for your thoughtful design and good-natured smile. Neither went unnoticed and both were appreciated. To Jane Willson, Andrea O'Connor and the team at Hardie Grant, thank you for your belief in this idea, bringing it so beautifully to print, and making dreams come true. Thanks also to Katrina O'Brien for your assiduous eye and astute word craft. And a special mention to Belinda Graham and Bianca Tzatzagos for your input and honesty, no matter the time of day. Also, to the magazine editors, who have made this wonderful writerly life possible. And to Deborah Bibby, for believing in me at the very start, and continuing to encourage me. This book embodies many lessons I've learnt from you. To my mum, for taking that plane trip down to Melbourne with my baby, and always being there for me and my family, as well as opening the door to your home so I could write – love knows no words. To Dad, Adam, Bruce, Tuula and John, for helping in many ways. Also, thank you Helen. The biggest thank you of all goes to Daniel – for your love, support, patience, meals, feedback, and not only holding the fort at home and Imprint House, but building them too. Lastly, to my children – Charlie, Sabina, Isis and Miles – home is where you are and, yes, the book is finally finished.

Published in 2018 by Hardie Grant Books,
an imprint of Hardie Grant Publishing

Hardie Grant Books (Melbourne)
Building 1, 658 Church Street
Richmond, Victoria 3121

Hardie Grant Books (London)
5th & 6th Floors
52–54 Southwark Street
London SE1 1UN

hardiegrantbooks.com

 A catalogue record for this
book is available from the
National Library of Australia

This Is Home
ISBN 978 1 74379 345 9

20 19 18 17 16 15 14 13 12 11

Publishing Director: Jane Willson
Managing Editor: Marg Bowman
Project Editor: Andrea O'Connor
Editor: Katrina O'Brien
Design Manager: Jessica Lowe
Designer: Evi O.
Photographer: Chris Warnes
Production Manager: Todd Rechner
Production Coordinator: Tessa Spring

All effort has been made to seek permission for the use
of quotes included in this book. The Publisher wishes
to thank the copyright holders for their permission
to reproduce material in this book.

Colour reproduction by Splitting Image Colour Studio

Printed in China by Leo Paper Products LTD.